D1298702

HUNTING

HUNTING

DAVID E. NEWTON

AN IMPACT BOOK

FRANKLIN WATTS

NEW YORK   CHICAGO   LONDON   TORONTO   SYDNEY

For Spec and Agnes,
with all my love!

Photographs copyright ©: North Wind Picture Archives: pp. 1, 2, 3, 4, 5 top, 5 center; New York Public Library, Picture Collection: p. 5 bottom; Photo Researchers Inc.: pp. 6 (Allen Cruikshank), 7 top (Len Rue, Jr.), 7 bottom, 11, 12 (all Leonard Lee Rue III), 8 bottom (Lynn McLaren), 9 top (Clem Haagner), 14 top (M. Wendler/Okapia); Alaska Division of Tourism: p. 8 top: The Wildlife Collection/Martin Harvey: p. 9 center; Comstock Photography/Bill Ervin: p. 9 bottom; UPI/Bettmann Newsphotos: pp. 10, 15, 16; Animals Animals/Len Rue, Jr.: p. 13; U.S. Fish & Wildlife Service/Mike Smith: p. 14 bottom.

Library of Congress Cataloging-in-Publication Data

Newton, David E.
   Hunting / David E. Newton.
      p.   cm. — (An Impact book)
   Includes bibliographical references and index.
   Summary: Examines the history, legal aspects, equipment, and various philosophies of hunting.
   ISBN 0-531-13022-3
   1. Hunting—Juvenile literature.   2. Hunting—United States—Juvenile literature.   [1. Hunting.]   I. Title.
   SK35.5.N48   1992
   799.2—dc20   92-24519   CIP   AC

CONTENTS

HUNTING

HUNTING
IN
HISTORY

The hunt was on! Org had found a young cave bear outside her den. He had called the tribe to help him kill the bear. Every person in the tribe was after the bear. Org waved a burning stick in the bear's face. Auk threw stones at her. Mub tried to hit the bear from behind with his heavy club. Gog shoved a long stick between her legs.

Finally the bear collapsed. Auk jumped on her back. He smashed the bear's skull with a heavy rock. The bear died at once. The hunt was over. The tribe would have enough meat to last at least a week. It would also use the bear's skin and fur for clothing.

HUNTING IN PREHISTORIC TIMES

The story describes one way historians believe that hunting was done by the earliest humans. There are no written records of human activities that long ago, but modern scientists have a number of ways of finding out what life might have been like back then. Archaeologists have uncovered the remains of communities that existed tens and hundreds of thousands of years ago. In many cases, these remains include the bones of animals killed during hunting expeditions. At Predmost, Czechoslovakia, scientists found the remains of more than one thousand mammoths and more that twenty-five thousand stone tools. A site in Stellmoor, Germany, revealed thirteen hundred reindeer antlers and forty axes made from antlers.[1]

The age of these communities can be determined by radioactive isotope dating. By counting the amount of radiation given off by various materials, scientists can tell how long the materials have been buried.

Scientists have also learned about primitive societies from cave paintings left by these societies. The paintings depict the animals hunted and the methods used in hunting. Drawings in the caves at Font-de-Gaume, France, show more than two hundred game animals, including eighty bison, twenty-three mammoths, forty horses, seventeen reindeer, and one bear. Other drawings show how fences, pits, and snow-banks were used to capture animals.[2]

Additional knowledge about this long-past age comes from studies of primitive societies in today's world. Scientists believe that the forms of hunting used in these societies are very much like those used in the distant past.[3]

One conclusion that scientists have drawn is that hunting is usually done by men. They believe that men are more likely to have the physical strength needed for hunting than are women. In addition, primitive societies often have difficulties maintaining stable populations. One way of doing so is for women to remain pregnant during most of their childbearing years, making them unsuited for hunting. However, scientists have also found some primitive societies in which women do the hunting. Among the Tiwi of northern Australia, for example, men hunt large animals while women hunt small and medium-size animals.[4]

THE EVOLUTION OF HUNTING

Scientists believe that the earliest ancestors of humans were probably vegetarians. The tooth structure of prehumans suggests that they lived primarily on nuts, berries, fruits, and plants that they could gather. Occasionally they might catch worms, a bird, a fish, or a small animal to add to their diet. That kind of diet is not very different from that of our primate cousins—the chimpanzees, gorillas, apes, and monkeys—even today.

Over time, meat became a more important part of the human diet. At first, humans may have simply stolen the meat killed by other, larger animals. Eventually, however, our ancestors developed the skill of hunting on their own. Over many thousands of years, humans evolved from rather timid plant eaters to the most efficient hunters in the animal world.

Unlike other meat eaters, humans have few natural assets as hunters. They don't run very fast, for example, nor do they have sharp claws or long, sharp teeth. Humans have become successful as hunters primarily because they have another asset: a well-developed brain.

With these brains, humans invented a number of tools and techniques that made them more efficient as hunters. At first, these tools were no more complex than the sticks and stones used by Org and his tribe. Even in those earliest days, however, humans used other techniques to kill their prey. For example, they built traps to snare their victims or dug pits in which to capture them.

One thing humans learned early was to work in

groups. For example, a group of people working together could hunt down a gopher. Some of them would block off all of the outlets to the gopher's hole except one. Then they would trample and beat on the ground, scaring the gopher out of its single open exit. As it left the hole, one man would kill the gopher with a rock.

Another example of group hunting was the practice of driving wild horses over a cliff. Members of a tribe would surround a group of wild horses near a cliff. Then they would shout, wave their arms, and set fires behind the horses. In a panic, the horses would run away from the noise and the fires and dash over the cliff. This practice is best known from remains found near the region of Soultre in France. Scientists believe that Stone Age hunters killed hundreds of thousands of wild horses by this method. Besides wild horses, cave bears, woolly rhinoceroses, mammoths, reindeers, and bison were the most popular prey of Stone Age humans.

HUNTING TOOLS

Humans have always shown great imagination in developing hunting weapons. One of the first of these weapons was the spear. The earliest form of the spear was probably nothing more than a sharpened stick. Later, a more advanced form of the weapon consisted of a sharpened stone attached to a long stick. The spear was to be the human's most effective killing device for tens of thousands of years.

New and better hunting devices were constantly being invented. The spear-thrower, for example, consisted of a short piece of wood held while tossing the spear. The extra length of wood increased the speed and force with which the spear could be thrown.

Over time, entirely new methods for killing animals were developed, including special throwing sticks like the boomerang, blowpipes equipped with poisoned arrows, baited traps, nooses, snares, and camouflaged pits.

No one knows when the first bow and arrow were invented. Some authorities think the weapon first appeared in northern Africa in late Paleolithic times, about ten thousand years ago.[5] By the Mesolithic Era (8000 B.C.–3000 B.C.), however, the bow and arrow were used everywhere in Europe. They replaced the spear as the most efficient hunting weapon and would remain so until the invention of the rifle in the fourteenth century.

THE BIRTH OF AGRICULTURE

One of the great turning points in human history was the invention of agriculture, about twelve thousand years ago. Humans learned how to grow the food they needed on a plot of land. They no longer had to travel great distances to collect the plants they needed for their food.

The domestication of animals occurred at about the same time. Studies of the ancient town of Shanidar in Iraq show clear signs of a sudden and dramatic change in about 9000 B.C. Instead of eating wild goats they had hunted, the people of Shanidar began eating sheep they had domesticated.[6] Within a relatively short time, humans had domesticated cows, sheep, goats, and pigs.[7] For the first time in history, meat-eating humans had an alternative to hunting. They could raise domesticated animals on a farm rather than hunt wild animals for food.

That change certainly did not make hunting obsolete. For a number of reasons, people continued to hunt. First, hunting was still the best way for many individuals to get meat for the dinner table. It was—

and still is—cheaper for many people to hunt than to maintain farm animals. Second, hunting became necessary to protect human communities and their animals from wild animals.

Third, hunting was still an important social activity. Remember how hunting was a communal activity among out earliest ancestors? For thousands of years, hunting had been more than just a way of getting food. It became a tradition, a social custom, a way of holding people together.

Finally, success in the hunt was still a matter of prestige. One way for an individual to prove his or her courage was to hunt down and kill another animal. Thus, domesticated animals might be able to provide humans with all of the meat they needed. But hunting had come to be important for other reasons too, reasons that had nothing to do with survival. It had become a social event and a form of recreation.

HUNTING AS A SPORT

The dawn of agriculture, therefore, created a new role for hunting. In addition to its traditional functions, it became a sport. The term *sport hunting* refers to an activity in which animals are pursued and killed not primarily to obtain food but for some other purpose. Throughout history, sport hunting has often been especially popular among the upper classes: the royalty, nobility, or very rich. These people owned most of the land and animals in an area. They had the time to go hunting and the money to pay for the equipment they needed. They controlled the right of hunting as they controlled many other rights in a country.

In ancient Egypt, for example, hunting and fishing were a special privilege of the ruling class. In fact, only the pharaoh was allowed to hunt certain animals such as the hippopotamus, lion, and wild bull.[8]

Engravings on temples, coffins, chests, and monuments often tell of the notable successes of Egyptian royalty. One such record describes how Amenophis III killed 102 lions in ten years. Another announces that the same king also killed 96 wild bulls in a herd of 170. Inscriptions on a set of 350 clay tablets from the year 1350 B.C. credit the pharoah Tuthmosis III with having killed 120 elephants in a single hunting expedition. In fact, the king probably did not kill all of those elephants by himself. As is often the case with such stories, the kills were probably those of the whole hunting party. Everyone realized that it was just a matter of good manners (and perhaps self-preservation) to credit all of the kills to the king.

Hunting was also popular among the Assyrians and Babylonians. Archaeologists have found many monuments describing the hunting expeditions of the royalty. In the seventh century B.C., for example, King Ashurbanipal called himself "the hunting king." One of his monuments carries the boast, "I killed the lion."[9]

In some societies, hunting became the special responsibility of a select group of men. Such was the case in the African kingdom of Benin. The most gifted young men of the tribe were selected for the hunting group. They were then trained to become very efficient hunters. Hunts conducted by this group were partly sport, partly religious, and partly social events.

The best members of the groups were allowed an even higher honor: to become elephant hunters. When a hunter in this group killed an elephant, one tusk went to the king. The hunter was allowed to keep the second tusk. For men of the Benin kingdom, being chosen as a hunter was the highest honor one could hope for.[10]

Hunting was also popular in Asia. One traditional legend, the Twelfth Tale of Jataka, tells of hunting in ancient India. It explains the Buddha's teachings about hunting.

The Buddha knew of the passion of Indian rulers for hunting. He was concerned about the number of animals killed and the methods used to kill them. In the Twelfth Tale, the Buddha teaches people that they must protect and preserve wild animals. It is wrong, he says, to slaughter game for the pure joy of killing.[11]

In China, hunting was both a sport and a form of military training. All hunting was under the control of the Ministry of War. The ablest of hunters became members of the emperor's archery unit.

Much of the emperor's hunting was done in one of his own private parks. One such park was about twenty-five miles square. It was stocked with animals brought in from all around the country. Official records describe one hunt in the park in 1120 B.C. in which the emperor's party killed "22 tigers, 2 wild cats, 5235 stags, 12 rhinoceroses, 721 yaks, 151 brown bears, 118 grizzly bears, 352 wild boars, 18 badgers, 16 elk, 50 musk deer, and 3508 Sika deer."[12]

Hunting has long tradition in the Western Hemisphere also. Some of the earliest firsthand reports about hunting in Middle America come from Spanish explorers to Central America and Mexico. They reported that "ordinary" people hunted primarily to get food for the table or to sell. But the nobility conducted hunts for pleasure. One story tells of the great emperor Montezuma taking twenty-five of his nobles with him to a special hunting area, where they killed birds with blowpipes that shot clay balls.[13] Another writer tells of great *battues* (group hunts) that took place in the fourteenth month of the Aztec year. The hunters were a tribute to the god of war, Uitzilopochtli, and the god of hunting, Mixcoatl. During a battue, warriors lined up "like a single length of rope" and drove deer, coyotes, and rabbits into the open. Anyone who killed a deer or a coyote was given a special gift by the emperor.[14]

A French historian of the late nineteenth century, Lucien Biart, provides much detail about the hunting techniques of the Aztecs. He says that the number of animals killed in battues was so large that the Spanish governor would not believe the stories until he had taken part in one himself. The battue to which he was taken ended in the capture of six hundred deer and wild goats, a hundred foxes, and "an incalculable number of hares and rabbits."[15]

Biart also describes some of the techniques used by Aztec hunters. For example, those who lived on a lake covered their heads with large gourds and floated out onto the water. They were able to sneak up on ducks and geese swimming in the lake, capture them by the feet, and drown them.[16]

HUNTING IN EUROPE

Until the seventh century, there were no hunting laws in Europe. All persons except slaves were allowed to hunt almost anywhere. Anyone who was permitted to carry a gun was also allowed to hunt. The leaders of German tribes in the fifth and sixth centuries, for example, had no special hunting privileges that were not available to other members of the tribe.[17]

One of the first hunting laws was published in the year 648. By this time, certain rulers had taken ownership of large stretches of land. They decided to restrict hunting on these land for their own use and that of the nobility. The 648 decree set aside the royal forests of Ardennes for the private use of King Dagobert.[18]

Over the next few centuries, many similar laws were published. The amount of land set aside for the ruling class became larger and larger. Penalties for illegal hunting by commoners became more and more severe. For example, one of Charlemagne's laws specified a fine of 60 schillings for anyone who entered a royal forest illegally. As a basis for comparison, it cost 1 schilling to purchase a cow at the time.[19]

As in earlier societies, hunting was a passion among European rulers. Charlemagne's son, Louis the Pious, is a typical example of this passion. One author claims that it seemed impossible that Louis "had any time at all to do anything but hunt. He hunted the stag until the start of the wild boar season and went hawking when there was nothing else to do; he was constantly on the move, from one end of his kingdom to the other, in search of as much variety as possible."[20]

Many similar stories could be told. Elector John George II of Saxony was said to have refused the crown of Bohemia in the seventeenth century because of his love of hunting. The deer in Bohemia were not as large as those in Saxony, he said, so he refused to leave his homeland. An indication of the elector's love of hunting is the report that he was credited with shooting 42,649 red deer in his lifetime.[21]

SOME TYPES OF GAME HUNTING

One of the most popular forms of hunting among the nobility was falconry. In this form of sport, a falcon was trained to attack and (sometimes) kill other birds. Falcons were trained by their masters to respond to commands as to where, when, and how to attack. One author has described the relationship between man and bird as "an advanced ballet in which the falcon was the prima ballerina and the falconer the choreographer."[22] Falconry probably originated in China in the sixth century B.C. and quickly spread to Japan, India, and the rest of Asia. Marco Polo told about hunting camps in Manchuria that held more than two thousand falconers.[23]

Falconry was brought to Europe in the third century A.D., but it did not become widely popular until the Middle Ages. When it did, the sport quickly spread through all of the courts of Europe. Women of the court were often as interested in the sport as the men were. Queen Elizabeth I (1558–1609) was fond of falconry and appointed another woman, Mary of Canterbury, as her Grand Master of the Hunt.[24]

Even the clergy were fascinated by falconry, as they were by other forms of hunting. Bishops often announced bans prohibiting priests from practicing falconry, but those bans were usually ignored. In fact, by some reports, priests sometimes brought their falcons to church and left them on the high altar during Mass.[25]

Perhaps the purest example of hunting as sport is fox hunting. A fox hunt begins when the Master of the Hounds welcomes his guests to the hunt. The guests may number from forty to eighty or more. The hunt is surrounded with a number of fixed customs, especially involving the type of clothing worn during the hunt.

The hunt begins when a pack of fifty or more dogs is released. The dogs set out in search of any fox in the area. Members of the hunt follow on horseback. When the dogs catch the fox, they are allowed to kill and eat it. For the hunters the point of the hunt is the excitement of the chase.

Fox hunting has been especially popular in Great Britain since 1750. By 1895, there were 323 hunting packs, with a total of 20,835 dogs, in the nation.[26] Even today, the sport is popular in both Great Britain and the United States among a small group of people who can afford the high cost of maintaining dogs and horses and dressing in the traditional fashion.

BIG-GAME HUNTING

Throughout history, the ultimate hunting experience has often been the hunt for big-game animals: elephants, lions, tigers, elk, buffalo, bear, and wild boar, for example. The most exciting hunting tales from ancient Egypt to modern times often describe the battle between a hunter and one of these animals.

Big-game hunting grew in popularity as Europeans settled both Africa and North America. Both continents appeared to have an endless supply of big game. At first, these animals were killed primarily for food. As the continents were settled, however, big-game hunting continued as a sport

In modern Africa, organized hunting expeditions have often been called safaris. The aim of a safari hunter was usually to bring home a trophy of his or her hunt: the tusks or foot of an elephant, the horn of a rhinoceros, the head of a lion or tiger, or the skin of an antelope.

Safari teams included hunters, guides, and bearers who carried everything needed for the weeks-long hunting trip. Many safari guides boasted of the number of big game they killed. I. A. Hunter, for example, claimed to have shot more than one thousand rhinoceroses and fourteen hundred elephants during his long career near the end of the nineteenth century. In one ninety-day period, he killed eighty-eight lions and ten leopards. His job was made somewhat easier by the fact that he did much of his shooting from a moving train.[27]

Big-game hunting eventually had a devastating effect on wildlife in Africa, Asia, and North America. According to one estimate, up to seventy thousand elephants alone were killed annually between 1850 and 1880 in East Africa. A total of more than 2 million were shot between 1880 and 1910 in that part of the continent. During this period, fourteen species of big game became extinct on the continent, at least partly as a result of hunting.[28]

When the first settlers landed in North America, they found a hunter's dream. An enormous variety and supply of animals of all kinds awaited them. As had always been the case, the hunt for these animals was often an economic necessity. It provided the food that settlers needed to survive. But hunting was also a sport. It provided the kind of recreation that had been enjoyed by the Egyptians, the Chinese, the Indians (of India), and the European ancestors of the new American nation.

HUNTING
IN
NORTH AMERICA

To the first Europeans arriving in North America, the continent seemed like a hunter's paradise. These men and women had just come from Europe, where game animals were scarce and protected by elaborate hunting laws and traditions. In their new nation, settlers found an abundance of game for the taking. One could literally walk out of the front yard and shoot a deer, a wild turkey, a waterbird, or small game.

Among the colonists, the primary purpose of hunting was survival. The birds and animals they killed were an important part of their diet during their difficult first years in the New World.

Occasionally, animals also were hunted for reasons of security. Individuals and government were sometimes concerned about the danger that some wild animals might pose to people and domestic animals. The fear of the gray wolf was an example. As early as 1630, the Massachusetts Bay Colony established a bounty on the gray wolf. It agreed to pay 1 cent for each wolf killed. This price tells us how many wolves must have lived in the area, since they were regarded so cheaply. In spite of its abundance, however, the wolf was hunted to its "utter destruction" in New England and eastern Canada by 1800, at least partly as a result of the bounty system.[1]

Colonists also found time to do some sport hunting. The most famous example of this form of recreation was the turkey shoot. Each person paid a fee to shoot and was allowed to take home any bird he or she killed. A writer of the time pointed out that "of course the poor shots pay for the turkeys which the good ones carry home."[2]

The philosophy of "every man a hunter" became an accepted part of American society. Indeed, some of the young nation's earliest heroes made their reputation by hunting. Daniel Boone was perhaps the most famous of these heroes. Boone spent the first thirty-six years of his life in North Carolina and Virginia as a farmer. Then, in 1769, he set out for the Kentucky frontier. He was driven by his love of hunting and of the free life in the untamed wilderness.

Over the next fifty years, Boone became an American folk hero. His hunting achievements, battles against the Native Americans, and political successes on the frontier were soon known throughout the nation. His accomplishments became larger than life, the ideal of a free existence in the natural world. They continued to inspire Americans for generations after his death.

Hunters like Daniel Boone became the subject of some of America's greatest early fiction. James Fenimore Cooper, for example, based his Leatherstocking tales—*The Deerslayer, The Last of the Mohicans, The Pathfinder, The Pioneer,* and *The Prairie*—on the lives and accomplishments of such men. These are the stories and role models with which untold numbers of young Americans grew up in the next century and a half.

HUNTING FOR PROFIT

Stories about Daniel Boone reflect his love of nature and his respect for wildlife. One can hardly imagine his taking part in a hunting party whose goal it was to kill as many animals as possible. Hunters like Daniel Boone presented an insignificant threat to the wildlife of North America. Indeed, a 1962 review of hunting in the United States noted that "advancing pioneers and sedentary farmers using game for their personal needs probably had little lasting effect on wildlife populations."[3] The report went on to acknowledge the effect of habitat loss in the decline of species. When pioneers moved into a new area, they cleared the land for farms and towns. Trees were cut down to make room for human communities. Forests disappeared at an alarming rate. Many animals lost the environment they needed to survive.

Still, habitat loss was not as important a factor in the loss of wildlife as were two other human activities: hunting for commercial profit and hunting for recreation. One of the first animals to experience the effect of market trappers and hunters was the beaver.

British settlers had come to North America expecting to make their fortunes. Soon they discovered that the northern colonies had only two major products worth harvesting: timber and fur-bearing animals. Among the most popular of those animals was the beaver.

Beaver fur was in great demand for the manufacture of hats. In fact, King Charles I had decreed in 1638 that all hats manufactured in England had to be made from beaver fur. That decree, one writer has pointed out, "was a severe blow to the North American beaver, but a mighty boost to the merchant class."[4]

At first, beavers were harvested (usually trapped) by colonists themselves. Before long, however, Native Americans were employed to kill the animals. The success of white man and Native American working together was little short of phenomenal. A Hudson Bay Company sale in November 1743, for example, included 26,750 beaver pelts. In another case, a shipment reaching the French port of La Rochelle included 127,080 beaver pelts.[5] By 1750 the kill of beaver in eastern North America had reached more than two million animals. In many regions of the United States and Canada, the animal had become extinct.[6]

Nor were beavers the only animals whose furs and skins were in demand. Otter, weasels, mink, marten, fisher, wolverine, raccoons, deer, wolves, and bears were also hunted for their pelts. Numbers like those for beaver pelts can also be cited for other fur-bearers. For example, the records for the year 1743 at La Rochelle also listed the pelts of 30,325 martens, 1,267 wolves, 12,428 otters, 110,000 raccoons, and 16,512 bears.[7] By 1800, the fur trade had become "the chief business of the colonies."[8]

Over time, wild animals also grew in popularity as a commercial source of meat. By the 1850s, many restaurants and large hotels were offering game as a gourmet item on their menus. Chicago's Palmer House hotel, for example, required a daily supply of at least a dozen different game animals.[9]

HUNTING FOR FUN

A second threat to wildlife came from hunters who carried sport hunting to an extreme. These hunters were not in the tradition of Daniel Boone, killing no more than a handful of animals because they needed the food or for the joy of the hunt. They were individuals who have been called "game hogs," whose goal it was to top some other hunter's record.

An example of the game hog might be Judge H. A. Bergen. Judge Bergen is reported to have shot sixty-four broadbill ducks, ninety-eight black ducks, and one Gadwall duck, all on a single day in the early 1900s, between 9 A.M. and 1 P.M.[10] Such slaughters of wildlife were not uncommon. Another writer has described annual hunts in the upper Mississippi valley during the nineteenth century: "[During] the spring shoots in the upper Mississippi valley, . . . a wagon load of plover and curlew, heaped higher than the sideboards, was considered a fair bag by the gentry of Omaha. If blazing away into the flocks filled the wagons up too soon, the bleeding pile was speedily dumped onto the prairie, there to rot, and the wagon loaded up all over again."[11]

Hunting books and magazines are filled with stories like these. The ultimate effect of such forms of hunting on wildlife is illustrated by the case of the passenger pigeon.

At one time, the passenger pigeon was so abundant that it seemed absolutely safe from destruction by humans. The report of a conservation committee organized to study the passenger pigeon insisted that the bird needed no protection from human hunters. The committee said that "no ordinary destruction can lessen them or be missed from the myriads that are yearly produced."[12]

Many observers reported seeing flocks so large that they would blot out the sun. When they roosted, trees looked as though they grew birds, not leaves, on their branches. At one nesting in Wisconsin in

1871, experts estimated that 136 million birds were present. When word of the nesting got out, hunters from all over the United States came to Wisconsin. Some were commercial hunters who hoped to make a profit on the birds they shot. Others were sport hunters who simply wanted to see how many birds they could kill.

In the end, millions of birds were killed. They were shot, trapped in nets, brought down by rocks and stones, and even captured and killed by hand. At first, commercial hunters were able to sell the birds they killed for 15 to 25 cents per dozen. Within a month, however, so many birds had been killed that they could no longer be sold at any price.[13]

The Wisconsin hunt of passenger pigeons was an extreme but not unusual example. Not even the apparently indestructible passenger pigeon could survive this type of onslaught. Less than thirty years after the Wisconsin hunt, the last passenger pigeon was killed in the wild. A captive bird, Martha, died in the Cincinnati Zoo in 1914. She was the last of her species on earth.

NATIVE AMERICANS AND THE HUNT

The hunting philosophies of European colonists and Native Americans were very different. The first white men in North America came from a long tradition that allowed hunting for both survival and sport. Some writers claim that European beliefs about hunting were influenced by Christian teachings. They point out that God has given humans dominion over other animals. In the Bible, God is quoted as ordering Adam to "be fruitful and multiply, and fill the earth and subdue it; and have dominion over the fish of the sea and over the birds of the air and over every living thing that moves upon the earth."[14] Thus, many Christians believe that plants and animals are placed here on earth for the pleasure and use of humans.

The attitude of Native Americans was quite different. They did not think of themselves as *above* nature but as *part of* it.[15] The totem pole is a concrete example of that philosophy. A *totem* is a group of people, spirits, and plants and animals that make up one large "family." A member of the Dakota tribe, for example, might also be a member of the coyote totem. Human and coyote were bound closely to each other. The coyote might even contain the spirit of one of the human's ancestors. Native Americans often apologized to the animals they killed. For example, hunters of the Abnaki tribe in Canada traditionally spoke to bears they had killed. "Do not be angry with us because we had to kill you," the hunters said. "You are wise, and you do see that our children are hungry. They love you, and invite you to enter their body. Is it not glory to be eaten by the chieftain's children?"[16]

In a letter to President Franklin Pierce in 1855, Chief Seathl (Seattle) of the Duwamish tribe in Washington state explained the difference between the way Native Americans and white men viewed nature. "The White man must treat the beasts of this land as his brothers. I am a savage and I do not understand any other way. . . . What is man without beasts? If all the beasts were gone, men would die from great loneliness of spirit, for whatever happens to the beasts also happens to the man."[17]

Because of this philosophy, Native Americans were less likely to kill animals purely for sport. They did, however, use animals for food, clothing, weapons, and other purposes. Furthermore, when it was necessary to kill an animal, they always tried to use *all* of the animal. The meat was eaten, skin and furs were made into clothing or housing, bones were used for weapons and tools, sinew became bowstings and ropes, and even teeth were valued as jewelry.[18]

Hunting patterns varied widely among Native Americans. In northern Canada, some Eskimo tribes used weapons and methods very similar to those of Stone Age people. They grew no crops and relied on hunting and fishing for almost all of their dietary needs. Their most important prey by far was the caribou, which they hunted with metal-tipped spears. About the only plant food the Eskimos ate was the partially digested plants found in the stomachs of the caribous they killed.[19]

Native Americans of the Middle West had a more complex hunting culture. They hunted deer, elk, bear, buffalo, and small game such as marten, rabbit, and sable. They also trapped beaver and fished.

In the West, Native Americans depended almost entirely on buffalo for their survival. In fact, a Kiowa legend explained the tribe's dependence on the buffalo this way: "Here are the buffalo. They are to provide you with clothing and food. But if one day you see the buffaloes disappear from the face of the earth, you will know that your end, too, has come."[20]

Many tribes had ceremonial dances to attract the buffalo. These dances often lasted several days and nights until buffalo were finally spotted by scouts.

In one form of buffalo hunting, groups of men covered themselves with coyote skins and quietly sneaked up on a herd. When a hunter got close enough, he killed an animal and marked it with his own identifying sign. Before white men arrived, the bow and arrow, spear, and knife were the weapons most commonly used in hunting. Successful hunters shared their prizes with all members of the tribe, including those families whose hunters had come home empty-handed.[21]

WESTWARD EXPANSION

Early settlers rapidly used up the natural resources around them. They cut down forests for lumber and to make room for farms. Then, when they needed more lumber or more land, they moved a few miles to the west. Similarly, farmers made little or no effort to maintain the soil on which their crops grew. When the soil was no longer productive, they moved on to new lands.

Thus it was with animal resources. When hunters could no longer find beaver, elk, deer, and other animals on the Eastern Seaboard, they moved west for better hunting. Typical of those who pushed the nation's frontier westward were the "mountain men," groups of men who traveled together, usually hunting beavers. They trapped in spring and fall, selling the pelts they got to large trading companies. The mountain men survived by hunting for their own food. Usual targets were buffalo, elk, deer, antelope, and bear, although panther and dog meat and beaver tail were regarded as special delicacies.[22]

Like the Native Americans around them, the mountain men learned to use every part of an animal, not only for food but also for clothing, tents, and other basic necessities. Like so many before them, they hunted to survive and to make a living.

The most popular target for human hunters on the Western frontier was the bison, better known as the buffalo. Like a number of other North American animals, the buffalo seemed to exist in countless numbers. Native Americans sometimes described a herd as a "great brown blanket" that moved slowly across the land.[23] One traveler wrote that "the black shaggy beasts continued to thunder past us in handfuls, in groups, in masses, in whole armies; for forty hours in succession we never lost sight of them, thousands upon thousands, tens of thousands upon tens of thousands, a numberless multitude of untamed creatures, whose meat, as we thought, would be sufficient to supply the wigwams of all Indians to all eternity."[24]

For a number of reasons, the King of the Plains rapidly became one of the most hunted animals in American history. For one thing, the buffalo were in direct competition with pioneers. They ate the grass that cattlemen needed for their own animals. Also, by their sheer numbers and size, the buffalo threatened to destroy almost any human construction they came across. For example, they found telegraph poles ideal for scratching their backs. Few poles survived this experience for very long, however.

Tales are also told of wagon trains that got caught in a buffalo stampede. All that remained in such a case, according to one author, was "the sorry mess that had once been human beings and splinters little larger than matchwood of their waggons [sic]."[25]

Pioneers also realized that destruction of the buffalo was an effective weapon in their battle against Native Americans, for whom the animals were a source of food, hide, fur, and other products.

At the same time, buffalo became a main source of food for the thousands of settlers moving west. They were accessible and easy to kill, often the main source of meat for travelers. Railroad companies hired hunters to provide buffalo meat for their construction crews. William F. "Buffalo Bill" Cody was perhaps the most famous of these hunters.

In addition, an eastern market for both buffalo

meat and buffalo fur and skins opened up. Delicacies such as buffalo tongue were especially in demand. Cody was only one of many hunters who supplied the animal to eastern markets as well as to the railroad companies. Cody claims at one point to have killed 4,280 buffalo in twelve months, for sale as meat.[26]

Hunting from trains was especially popular. Some railroad companies ran special excursions, on which every hunter was guaranteed the opportunity of seeing and shooting at buffalo.

Men from all over the world journeyed to the American West to hunt buffalo. The buffalo was especially popular among European nobility, but "emigrants, merchants, and any old traveler also joined in the sport," according to one authority.[27]

The final result was not hard to predict. Between 1872 and 1874, over a million buffalo were killed each year in the southern part of their range. Only ten years later, there were virtually no buffalo left anywhere in the West. Nearly 10 million had been killed.[28]

A similar drama was played out in Canada. There, the woodland caribou was hunted for food and sport, as was the buffalo in the United States. As in the American West, travelers from Europe relished a sport that no longer existed anywhere at home. On one not unusual hunting expedition, an English visitor was credited with killing 120 caribous in a single day.[29]

The slaughter of the caribou troubled Samuel Hearne, a Canadian naturalist. Hearne acknowledged that "the great destruction of the deer . . . is almost incredible," but he was assured by the Native Americans that "the deer are as plentiful now as they have ever been." On this basis, he doubted that hunting could have any long-term effect on the caribou.

Hearne was wrong, however. By the 1890s, intensive hunting had largely brought about the extinction of the caribou in most of its natural habitat.

PROTECTION FOR GAME ANIMALS

The end of the nineteenth century also saw the end of the American frontier. Pioneers had pushed as far west as they could go, to the Pacific Ocean. In the process of settling the West, they had also decimated that region's wildlife populations. By destroying natural habitat and through hunting, humans had wiped out a number of game animals that a century earlier had been abundant.

Many hunters were troubled at this turn of events. The United States had rapidly become like European nations. Game was scarcer and scarcer. If sport hunting were to survive, something would have to be done to protect the remaining populations of game animals.

The protection ultimately provided took three forms: (1) the enactment of stronger hunting laws and the more vigorous enforcement of these laws; (2) the establishment by federal, state, and local governments of areas where hunting was carefully controlled; and (3) the creation of privately owned game preserves.

Hunting laws had existed in the United States since colonial times. But these laws were rarely enforced. One nineteenth-century writer had observed that "the game laws of most States are a mere bagatelle [trifle] that no one regards; in other words, they are all a dead letter." [30]

After 1900, that situation began to change. Federal, state, and local governments began to adopt an increasing number of hunting laws. These laws generally had one common aim: to guarantee that some control was maintained over the size of game populations. The philosophy was to guarantee that at least some hunters would have a chance of going after the game animals they wanted to hunt, then and in the future. In addition, game agencies began to enforce existing game laws and regulations much more aggressively than they had in the past.

Game was also protected by the creation of certain areas where hunting was entirely prohibited and other areas where it was carefully limited. For example, hunting was absolutely prohibited in the nation's national parks and monuments and in most state parks. On the other hand, hunting was allowed in national and state forests. However, the number of hunters permitted and the length of the hunting season was carefully controlled. Game officers made sure that no species was threatened as a result of overhunting.

These policies made possible the survival and growth of many formerly endangered animals. Toward the end of the nineteenth century, for example, there may have been no more than a few hundred buffalo left in the American West. Eventually that number rose to tens of thousands. The reason for this reversal was the protection provided to the animals in Yellowstone National Park and other protected areas.

The recovery of the deer population in Pennsylvania is another great success story. By the beginning of the twentieth century, deer had been completely eliminated from the state. But then the state's governor, Gifford Pinchot, established a number of game preserves where deer were reintroduced and hunting was not allowed. Eventually, the number of deer grew so large that hunting was once again permitted. Today, more deer hunting licenses are issued in Pennsylvania than in any other state of the Union.

PRIVATE GAME PRESERVES

Even before 1900, many private citizens had seen the "handwriting on the wall" regarding hunting. They feared that there would soon be no place in the United States that hunters could go to enjoy their sport. As a result, people and organizations began to buy up lands to use for hunting. The lands were reserved for use by members of a hunting club or by anyone willing to pay to hunt on the land.

Many observers think that private game preserves represent the most important trend in hunting in North America today. For example, although there are fewer than 2 million acres of federal and state lands in Texas on which hunting is permitted, there are more than 30 million acres of private lands where one can pay to hunt.[31] Today, owners tempt hunters with advertisements that promise "jeep shuttles" to the fields, "heated, elevated [hunting] blinds," and "meals served" during the hunting expedition. Hunters are charged a flat fee for each day on the preserve (normally $25 to $50) or a fee for each animal killed. Owners make sure that the preserves are well stocked and that animals are well maintained. They do their best to see that no hunter goes home without a trophy.[32]

Some game preserves specialize in unusual ("exotic") game animals that are not native to the United States. Among the exotics that have been imported to stock these preserves are eland, oryx, impala, greater kudu, ibex, springbok, European boar, and tahr. The charge for killing one of these animals ranges from about $350 to $750.[33]

Private game preserves have become the subject of much controversy. On the one hand, these private lands provide the last opportunity that many Americans hunters will have to experience the thrill of bagging big game that was once commonplace in this country only a century ago. On the other hand, they raise new issues about the rights of all Americans and Canadians to hunt. One hunting writer, Keith McCafferty, has described the growth of private game preserves as a "commercialization of our wildlife resources." Writing in the hunting and fishing magazine *Field and Stream,* he calls this trend "the most important issue that sportsmen of our century have ever faced." He predicts that hunting in North America will become similar to hunting in Europe, where only the wealthy can pay the high cost of hunting on private game reserves.[34]

McCafferty warns that in future generations, success for hunters "will not depend upon how well they train their dogs or point their shotguns as much as how deeply they are able to reach into their pockets." In the more populous regions of the West, in states like Texas, New Mexico, and Colorado, he says, "that day has come."[35]

That reality is reflected in how-to articles that now appear in many hunting magazines. For example, a 1990 article on deer hunting in the western states warned readers about the problems of finding land on which to hunt. "Hunt clubs, outfitters, and groups of hunters lease practically every acre of private land," the author says. The hunter *can* find public lands on which to hunt, he agrees, but the task is not an easy one. "A good map is required to ensure that private lands aren't being trespassed," he warns.[36]

The debate over game preserves reminds us how much hunting in North America has changed in three centuries. In many ways, modern American hunters share much with their colonial ancestors. In other very important ways, however, hunting today is a new, challenging, controversial activity throughout the continent. One of the major sources of disagreement is the subject of wildlife management. Should those who are interested in hunting be allowed to control the number of game animals in North America? Or is the attempt to manage wildlife for the sake of hunting an unfair and immoral activity?

WILDLIFE MANAGEMENT

The actions taken to protect game animals in the early 1900s were part of a broader movement to save North America's natural resources. In addition to wildlife, other resources, such as trees, soil, minerals, and water, were rapidly being depleted. Many Americans and Canadians believed that the continent's vast natural resources could be saved only by vigorous action. This movement became known as the conservation movement.

The term *conservation* refers to any activity to protect some natural resource from overuse. The purpose of conservation activities is to make sure that a natural resource, such as game animals, will survive for many generations into the future.

An important figure in the early conservation movement was Theodore Roosevelt, later the twenty-sixth president of the United States. Roosevelt was an avid hunter, in both North America and Africa. He wrote a number of books describing his experiences and the joys of hunting. Before he became president, he was a founding member of the Boone and Crockett (B&C) Club, an organization of very wealthy men interested in hunting and conservation. Some purposes of the B&C Club were to "promote manly sport with the rifle, to encourage exploration of wild country, to lobby for game laws, and to foster inquiry into the natural history of game animals."[1] Once he became president, Roosevelt worked aggressively to set aside land for the protection of wildlife. Eventually he declared more than 16 million acres of public land to be wildlife reserves.[2]

Roosevelt's action epitomized the activities of the newfound wisdom of the conservation movement. Humans were going to have to become more active in managing the continent's wildlife. If hunting and development were allowed to continue without control as in the past, a large part of the nation's wildlife resources were doomed.

THE HISTORY OF WILDLIFE MANAGEMENT

The science dealing with the conservation of wild animals is known as *wildlife management:* all methods used by humans to control the number of animals in an area. As an example, a state might decide that there are too many coyotes living within its borders and therefore declare an open hunting season on coyotes. When enough coyotes had been killed by hunters, the hunting season could be called off.

The concept of wildlife management is not a new one. Humans have been practicing the science—without calling it that—since the beginning of recorded history. Rulers have often announced regulations designed to limit the hunting of certain types of animals. The objective of these regulations was to ensure that enough of the population would survive for hunting in the future.

For example, Marco Polo told of bans on the hunting of game animals between March and October in the Mongol empire of Kublai Khan. This ban protected animals during their breeding season. The Khan also provided food and cover for the animals, improving their chances of survival.[3]

Wildlife management has been practiced aggressively in Europe for many hundreds of years. There, wildlife began to disappear centuries ago. The very small numbers of game animals that remain on the continent are all carefully managed in small, protected reserves. Hunting of the animals is also controlled and limited to those who can afford to pay for the privilege.

African and Asian nations have only recently begun to practice wildlife management. Until the mid-twentieth century, supplies of lions, elephants, tigers, rhinoceroses, and other game animals seemed to be limitless, as had once been the case in North America. But some Asian and African nations have begun to worry about the massive loss of these animals. And with that concern has come the practice of wildlife management on those continents also.

Wildlife managers can list many examples of the success of their craft. One of the best known has been the reestablishment of the wild turkey in the United States. When the first Europeans arrived, there may have been 10 million wild turkeys in North America. In the early nineteenth century, some observers reported seeing a thousand turkeys a day.[4]

But, like other wildlife, wild turkeys were shot and trapped indiscriminately. By the end of the nineteenth century, they had been totally eliminated from the New England States, Michigan, Wisconsin, and Minnesota. They were close to extinction in many other parts of North America.[5]

Vigorous efforts to protect the wild turkey began in the 1930s. Restrictive hunting laws were passed, and wildlife managers began restocking areas where turkeys had disappeared. Slowly the bird returned to much of its previous habitat. Between 1970 and 1982, for example, the number of wild turkeys killed in Michigan grew nearly twentyfold, from 91 to 1,760.[6]

Traditional concepts of wildlife management began to change in the 1930s. Some scientists began to suggest that wildlife management should involve more than setting aside game preserves for animals. A leader in this movement was Aldo Leopold, a naturalist, ecologist, and forester who, late in life, was appointed professor of forestry at the University of Wisconsin.

Leopold argued that nature should be studied and managed *as a whole*. Suppose one wanted to control the number of mule deer in an area. Controlling the number of deer shot by hunters with laws was only one method—and a crude one at that, he said—for achieving this objective. A more complete approach would be to study the food the deer eat, the diseases from which they suffer, their breeding patterns, their natural predators, and other factors that affect the size of the deer population. Management of the deer population would then involve the manipulation of one or more of these factors. Leopold's ideas were not widely accepted until many years later.

THE GOALS OF WILDLIFE MANAGMENT

Modern wildlife management has three major objectives:

1. To guarantee that there will be enough game animals to satisfy the needs of the nation's hunters.
2. To protect humans, land, and domestic animals from predators.
3. To protect endangered species.

Before the 1960s, by far the most important item on the above list would have been the first, since wildlife management grew up primarily as a means of maintaining a dependable supply of game animals for hunters. For example, a 1962 report on hunting by the University of Michigan explained that "most State game agencies have the objective of managing a variety of game populations so as to provide for quality public recreation by the licensed hunter."[7] By almost any measure, hunter "satisfaction" is still the most important objective of wildlife management.

Predator control (item 2 above) has always been practiced by humans to protect themselves and their property from wild animals. The practice was seldom a very scientific one, however. Farmers shot foxes that stole their chickens, and ranchers killed coyotes that ate their lambs.

Predator control has become a more important and more scientific activity in North America in the past century. As population grows, humans take over more land. Wild animals are displaced and deprived of their food. They tend to come into contact more often with human communities. Thus, we are no longer surprised by reports of bears that wander into remote towns.

As a consequence, predator control has become a major wildlife management activity for state and federal governments. At the national level, predator control is carried out under the Department of Agriculture's Animal Damage Control (ADC) program. Table 1 lists the number of animals killed intentionally and by accident under the ADC program in 1988.

Protection of endangered species is a recent goal of wildlife management. Until the 1960s, few people seemed to care that some animals (and plants) were being driven to extinction by human activities. Now

TABLE 1		

NUMBER OF ANIMALS KILLED BY THE U.S. DEPARTMENT OF AGRICULTURE'S ANIMAL DAMAGE CONTROL PROGRAM IN 1988

Animals	Intentionally Killed	Accidentally Killed
MAMMALS		
Coyote	76,033	17
Skunk	15,239	102
Beaver	9,143	28
Raccoon	5,348	1,117
Opossum	5,329	505
Fox	5,195	1,155
Bobcat	1,163	63
Badger	939	555
Porcupine	799	935
Nutria	612	21
Prairie dog	538	0
Rat/mouse	505	0
Hog (wild)	392	17
Muskrat	323	63
Black bear	289	2
Marmot	258	0
Mountain lion	203	4
Russian boar	192	5
Rabbit	186	231
Domestic cat	178	104
Ground squirrel	159	24
Domestic dog	151	393
Javelina	0	764
BIRDS		
Blackbird	4,453,842	1
Pigeon	7,982	0
Egret	6,729	0
Others	2,398	342

Cited in Michael Satchell, "The American Hunter under Fire,"
U.S. News & World Report, February 5, 1990, p. 37.

more of us are willing to acknowledge that *all* species deserve our consideration and protection.

THE METHODS OF WILDLIFE MANAGEMENT

In its earliest years, wildlife management could hardly have been called a science. The methods used were simple and straightforward. One technique was to set aside areas where hunting was not allowed. An important reason for creating North America's national parks, for example, was to provide safe havens for game animals.

That approach has been continued and expanded throughout this century. Today, all of the nation's more than 325 national parks and monuments are off limits to hunting. In addition, the U.S. Congress has established a system of 435 wildlife refuges. The purpose of these refuges was, in theory, to provide sanctuaries for a wide variety of wildlife. In fact, a majority of the refuges are no longer safe places for animals. The U.S. Fish and Wildlife Service (FWS) has now opened 256 of the 435 refuges to hunting as a form of wildlife management. The FWS argues that hunting is a legitimate tool for controlling the number of animals in the refuges.[8]

Hunting laws are another method of managing wildlife. What wildlife managers try to do is to decide on the optimum number of game animals for a particular area. They might decide, for example, that the maximum number of healthy elk that can live in Jones County is 250. If the herd grows larger than 250, they can allow enough hunting to reduce the elk herd to its optimum size.

Hunting laws normally specify the number of days an animal can be hunted, the age and sex of animals that can be killed, the total number of animals that can be taken in a season, and so on. Wildlife managers try to set these numbers based on the most desirable effect they will have on a game population.

Over the years, wildlife managers have become better at setting hunting limits. They have found ways to count the number of game animals in an area and the number killed each year by hunters. Still, this aspect of wildlife management is an inexact science. There are so many factors influencing the size of a game population that setting hunting laws still involves a lot of guessing.

Another tool of wildlife management is predator control. Under normal circumstances, the number of elk in Jones County is partially determined by the number of their predators that also live there. The more wolves and coyotes, the fewer elk. The fewer wolves and coyotes, the more elk. One way for wildlife managers to increase the supply of game animals, then, is to eliminate their predators.

And that is one thing wildlife managers have been very successful in doing. Wolves, coyotes, and other predators are disliked by many groups of people: wildlife managers (often), farmers, ranchers, and people who live in remote areas. We should hardly be surprised, then, by endless stories of predator extermination throughout North America. Note (in Table 1), for example, that far more coyotes were killed in the U.S. ADC program in 1988 than all other animals combined.

Similarly, the number of blackbirds killed in the program is very large. That number reflects two facts. First, the term *blackbird* is used for a great variety of birds, including grackles, cowbirds, red-winged blackbirds, and even crows and starlings.[9] Second, most farmers regard blackbirds as serious pests. They eat millions of dollars of sprouting corn and rice every year. The government carries out vigorous efforts, therefore, to destroy these animals.

The extermination of predators has provided an abundance of game for hunters, but it has also presented new problems for wildlife managers. For example, in the absence of nearly all predators, the number of white-tailed deer in the United States has mushroomed by 12 million since the early 1900s.[10] Even vigorous hunting has had little long-term effect on the deer population. It is no longer uncommon to hear about deer wandering into private gardens, across golf courses, and through community parks.

Another example of the effect of predator control occurred in 1990. The buffalo herd in Yellowstone National Park had grown too large for the amount of land available in the park. In addition, the buffalo's natural predators had all been exterminated by wildlife managers. As spring approached, some of the excess animals wandered across park boundaries into southern Montana, looking for food. Once outside the park, the buffalo became fair game for hunters. Having grown up with no fear of humans, the buffalo did not run from hunters. In all, 569 of them were shot dead, most at nearly point-blank range.

For some wildlife managers today, the vision of wildlife management presented by Aldo Leopold many years ago is a goal toward which they strive. A glimpse of the table of contents of a currently popular wildlife management textbook reveals the range of topics with which the subject can deal: ecosystems and natural communities, population ecology, animal behavior, food and cover, water resources, soils and farmland, rangeland, forest management, wildlife diseases, predators and predation, hunting and trapping, urban wildlife, exotic wildlife, and endangered species.[11]

Yet wildlife management today is pretty much

the way it has always been. Wildlife managers acknowledge that the role of hunting in controlling game populations is often unclear. Some studies show, for example, that the size of game populations is roughly the same with or without hunting.[12] Nonetheless, wildlife managers continue to depend heavily on hunting as a tool of control. As one author has written, "For better or worse, regulated hunting has become our nation's primary wildlife-management tool."[13]

CONTROVERSIES SURROUNDING WILDLIFE MANAGEMENT

The life of a wildlife manager is not an easy one. It seems that almost everyone can find some objection to raise about the way a wildlife manager does his or her job. Observers from all parts of society seem to agree with the observation that "most wildlife management is wildlife mismanagement."[14]

One controversy simply has to do with the language used by wildlife managers. Wildlife management often requires that animals be killed, but managers tend to avoid using the word *killing* whenever possible. They talk about "harvesting" or "culling" animals or about "utilizing a resource." Hunters also tend to use terms that are less direct than the word *killing*. They may refer instead to "taking" or "bagging" an animal.

Critics say that using this kind of neutral terminology has two effects. First, it may help wildlife managers and hunters avoid dealing with what, for many of them, is an apparently unpleasant reality. Second, it makes the act of death seem somewhat less terrible for nonhunters and perhaps for hunters too. One writer claims that "hunters are increasingly relying upon their spokesmen and supporters, state and federal game managers and wildlife officials, to employ the drone of a solemn bureaucratic language . . . to assure the non-hunting public (93 percent!) that there's nothing to worry about."[15]

Critics of wildlife management also complain about the concept of "favored species." That term refers to the fact that wildlife policies tend to encourage the growth of some species, often at the expense of other species.

For example, deer, elk, and moose are game animals favored by many hunters. Therefore, wildlife managers tend to follow practices that increase the numbers of these animals. To do so, they may have to exterminate other animals—wolves and coyotes, for example—that prey on favored species. Indeed, the population explosion of white-tailed and mule deer is largely a result of the extermination by wildlife managers of the deer's natural predators.

Critics feel that more equal protection should be given to all species. John Grandy, a vice-president of the U.S. Humane Society, asks, "What is logical about aggressively poisoning egg-eating predators—fox, mink, coyote, raccoon—at some refuges to help increase duck populations and then allow hunters to shoot the ducks?"[16]

Some experts recommend the abolition of certain wildlife management techniques. For example, habitat management techniques such as building ponds for waterfowl and clearing brush for deer may favor the population growth of these species, but they play havoc with others that lose the land and food they need to survive. Elimination of such techniques would provide all species with a more equal chance of survival.

There is an important and sometimes hidden assumption behind many of these protests. That assumption is that game animals are no more worthy of protection than are other animals. People who like to hike in the woods and go bird-watching also have the right to enjoy animals. Bird-watchers, for example, like to watch birds such as ducks, geese, and cranes that are favored by hunters and therefore protected by wildlife managers. But they also like to watch other kinds of birds, like robins, wrens, and thrushes, that hunters are not interested in and that therefore are not protected by wildlife management programs. Critics say that songbirds that are not of interest to hunters and wildlife managers are entitled to as much protection as deer. Sara Vickerman of the Defenders of Wildlife, for example, would prefer to see a more "coherent systematic approach to preserve habitat and prevent massive extinctions of plant and animal life."[17] This view reflects the opinion that the whole focus of wildlife management, as it is often practiced, is wrong. Wildlife managers should be less concerned with the fact of individual species and more with entire ecosystems.

Critics are especially angry about government policies that allow hunting on wildlife refuges. They claim that Congress created wildlife refuges to provide safe areas for animals. As Representative Bill Green (R-NY) has said, "There ought to be some places that are kept apart from man's predation."[18]

But since the 1960s, more and more refuges have been opened to hunting. More than half of the nation's 435 refuges now belong in this category. The result is that wild animals are being killed in the very areas set aside for their protection. According to Jennifer Lewis of the U.S. Humane Society, "more than 400,000 refuge animals each year are killed by hunters and trappers, and millions of birds are killed by poisoning attributed to lead shot. In addition, hunting disrupts other recreational uses of the refuges."[19]

Many wildlife managers disagree with this criticism. They point out, to begin with, that hunting on certain refuges is entirely legal. One reason to permit hunting, they say, is that it provides an effective and essential method of population control for many game animals.[20]

Furthermore, they argue that hunting is a reasonable recreational activity that is as worthwhile as bird-watching, hiking, and other wilderness activities. Noreen Clough of FWS says that hunting on refuges "is a legitimate recreation where it can be performed without detriment to other populations and where adequate funds are available."[21]

Frank Dunkle, former director of FWS, also responds to the critics of wildlife refuge hunting. "If you're worried about creating a disturbance," he suggests, "then keep everybody off the refuges. A guy waltzing through the brush disturbing animals with a camera is as bad as shooting, sometimes."[22]

Many hunters are no less angry at wildlife managers, but for different reasons. Most often, they see managers "caving in" to soft-hearted, fuzzy-thinking environmentalists who don't understand the value of hunting as a wildlife management technique. Hunting magazines often carry stories that illustrate how "dime-store ecologists," "strange rookies into wildlife management," and "amateur crusaders" who "love animals to death"[23] interfere with the most effective form of wildlife management known: hunting. One writer describes the way these "amateur crusaders" influence wildlife management practices by appealing to the public's love of animals. He concludes that "like political campaigns, wildlife management these days is often governed more by idealogues and hype than biologists and science. It's a pity, but that's how it is."[24]

Other critics claim that wildlife managers are doing too little to help hunters. Conservation writer

George Reiger is especially critical of government bureaucracies. He points out, for example, that government agencies often work at cross purposes. While the Soil Conservation Service is trying to drain wetlands as fast as it can in order to make new farmland, the Fish and Wildlife Service is working to maintain wetlands for waterfowl.

"State forestry and wildlife agencies are so locked into bureaucratic forms and procedures," he writes, "they're frequently unable to rally to common sense."[25] As a result, Reiger argues, many wildlife management agencies simply have nothing of value to offer landowners. Reiger is especially concerned about the status of small-game hunting in the East. Wildlife managers brag of their success in saving the wild turkey and the white-tailed deer, he says, but they ignore the "catastrophic declines" of other small-game populations. As more and more land is lost to development, wildlife managers could be helping to maintain these dwindling populations, Reiger says. Instead, the only help private landowners get from managers is "brochures telling them what they already know."[26]

In the West, the biggest battle involves private game reserves. More and more, the tendency is for landowners to close their property to the general public and allow only private hunting for a fee. In Montana alone, for example, nearly six hundred landowners are converting fifteen thousand square miles of their property to game farms. More that three hundred thousand head of elk, buffalo, and bighorn sheep will be stocked by these farmers.[27]

Government wildlife managers do not have direct control over these private reserves. However, they are in an excellent position, Reiger argues, to give advice about the development of private reserves. Managers should be willing to "contribute their knowledge to benefit wildlife on private lands."[28] In addition, he says, they should be "constantly before their legislatures" trying to support and encourage this new direction for hunting.[29] Few wildlife managers agree with this role, Reiger says. Instead, they tend to view colleagues who work with private reserves as "traitors."[30] This attitude is wrong, he believes. Fee hunting is here to stay. That may be too bad, but it's a fact of life.

The title of Reiger's article, "The Resource Revolution," illustrates the critical change that has taken place in North American hunting patterns. As the twenty-first century dawns, hunting is no longer the wide-open pursuit it was in the eighteenth and nineteenth centuries. Today a hunter's activities are much more closely controlled by laws and regulations designed to ensure a lasting supply of game animals for future generations.

HUNTING LAWS
AND
REGULATIONS

As far back as one can go in human history, authorities have been making laws about the hunting of animals. One wildlife management textbook suggests that the first "game policy" to appear in writing may be a passage from the Bible, in Deuteronomy 22:6.[1] That verse teaches that "if thou find as thou walkest by the way, a bird's nest in a tree, or on the ground, and the dam sitting upon the young or upon the eggs: thou shalt not take her with young." The regulation was apparently designed to protect female birds from being killed and destroying the next generation of animals.

Game laws became important relatively early in the history of Europe. Royalty claimed ownership not only of huge stretches of land but also of the wildlife living on the land. Rules decreed which animals could be hunted, when, and for how long. Those regulations normally did not apply to royalty or nobility.

Such regulations were often the cause of conflict between peasant and nobility. For peasants, hunting could be a matter of survival. It was almost the only way they could get meat for their diet. They could see the abundance of game in the king's forests, but they were severely restricted in their access to that game. The unauthorized taking of an animal from royal lands was often punished by death.

The tales of Robin Hood reflect this battle over hunting rights. Robin battled for the right of peasants to hunt, while his adversary, the sheriff of Nottingham, attempted to uphold royal privileges.

LAWS IN EUROPE AND NORTH AMERICA

Until quite recently, hunting laws in Europe and North America have been quite different. In Europe, wild animals have always been regarded as the property of the person on whose land they live. For example, a person might own ten thousand acres of land where deer, elk, and boar roam. That person legally owns the deer, elk, and boar as well as the land.

In North America, people can own land but not wild animals. A Montana rancher might hold the deed to ten thousand acres of rangeland, but the wild animals that live on that land belong to the people of the United States. Government agencies are responsible for how those animals are used.

Historically, therefore, hunters in North America have had primarily two choices. First, they could hunt on any public land that was not closed to hunting. Second, they could ask permission of a landowner to hunt the animals that lived on his or her private property.

Traditionally, the custom has been for landowners to allow hunters to travel across and hunt on their lands. Until recently, only a small fraction of landowners posted "No Trespassing" signs on their property, preventing hunters from using the land. Prohibited lands came to be known, therefore, as "posted" lands.

In the past few decades, that pattern has begun to change. Open space has been developed. Forests have been cut down. Suburbs have expanded into rural areas. Many people have decided they do not want hunters wandering through their fields. As a result, more and more landowners have "posted" their property. Hunters are finding it increasingly difficult to locate areas where they can hunt.

Because of this trend, hunters often have a third option available to them today: paying for the privilege of hunting on private lands. Sometimes the hunter pays simply for the right to be on a person's land. The wild animals on the land may be public property, but if the hunter can't get to them, he or she can't hunt them.

Other times, the hunter pays to hunt animals that a landowner has purchased and maintained on his or her land. These are not wild animals that belong to the general public but the landowner's personal property. As such, he or she can charge people a fee to hunt them. Private game preserves are examples of such lands.

STATE GAME LAWS

Whether hunters hunt on public or private lands, they are subject to specific game laws and regulations. Historically, in the United States, these laws have been the responsibility of the individual states. The earliest of these laws were passed within a few years of the settlement of Massachusetts and Virginia. The Massachusetts Bay Colony established the first law limiting the times at which deer could be hunted in 1694.[2]

The purpose of state game laws is to allow hunters to kill a certain number of game animals without endangering the survival of those animals. One job of wildlife managers is to determine what that "certain number" of animals will be each year. In some years, game animals may be abundant. Then hunters will be allowed to kill a greater number of the animals. In other years, a population may be small. Then hunting will be severely restricted. For this reason, the specific details of hunting laws change from year to year.

For example, the western states experienced a serious drought during the late 1980s and early 1990s. Many game animals perished because they could not find enough to eat. As a result, wildlife managers reduced the number of hunting permits awarded. In states like Arizona, Nevada, and California, the number of deer permits were cut back each year the drought was extended.

Other factors determined the number of permits issued also. In 1989, for example, the state of Utah banned the hunting of elks more than one year old in three parts of the state. They wanted to establish a population of older elks that would be prized as trophies by hunters. Also, they thought a larger number of elks would provide new recreational opportunities for wildlife photographers and other nonhunters who enjoy the wilderness.

Laws also differ from state to state. In locations where an animal is abundant, laws are likely to allow liberal hunting. In places where the same animal is rare, laws may prevent its hunting entirely. As an example, the state of Maine limited hunters to four cottontail rabbits per day in 1991. But the state of Arizona, where rabbits are more abundant, allowed hunters to take ten rabbits per day.

It would be impossible to discuss state game laws in any detail in this book. In any one state, those laws may take up many pages of text. In California, for example, forty-one distinct regions are set aside for deer hunting alone. A specific quota has been established for the number of deer that can be killed in each section. Special rules may also apply to some of these areas.

Laws and regulations usually deal with a number of different hunting conditions, including (1) open and closed season, (2) types of weapons that can be used, (3) age and sex of the animal, and (4) bag limits.

The terms *open* and *closed* season refer to times when an animal may or may not be hunted. For example, the open season on raccoons in Colorado in 1990–91 was between January 1 and December 31 1990.[3] That is, raccoons could be hunted at any time during the year. In Michigan, the open season on raccoons ran from November 15, 1990, to January 31, 1991. And in Maine, the open season lasted from October 22 to December 31, 1990. In contrast, Montana is one of the states that has a closed season all year long on the protected gray wolf.

The vast majority of hunting today is done with guns, usually rifles and shotguns. But some hunters prefer to use other types of weapons. The most popular weapon after guns is the bow and arrow. Bow-and-arrow hunters list a number of reasons for preferring their weapon over guns. Some come to hunting after originally having become interested in archery. Others enjoy the fact that, since many states have separate seasons for hunting with guns and for hunting with bow and arrow, they can take part in a double hunting season. Another attraction seems to be that landowners are sometimes more willing to allow bow-and-arrow hunters than gun hunters to use their land. They seem to believe that bow-and-arrow hunting is safer than gun hunting. Finally, bow-and-arrow hunters usually feel that their sport requires greater skill than does hunting with a gun.

Old-fashioned guns, such as muzzle-loaders, have

also come back into use by some hunters. A muzzle-loader takes a fairly long time to load, and a hunter normally gets only one shot at an animal. People who use muzzle-loaders like the experience of using simpler weapons popular many years ago. One muzzle-loader hunter has claimed that "these rifles are just so pretty and nostalgic that they've become impossible to resist." He warns, however, that muzzle-loader hunters must become accustomed to a whole new set of problems including "limited effective ranges, . . . and increased probability of misfires . . . the painstaking business of loading and priming, not to mention all the stuff you have to carry [such as] powder horns and a possibles bag filled with patches, balls, caps, powder measures, ball starters, nipple wrenches, nipple picks, cleaning jags, ball pullers, patch pullers, and a couple of other odds and ends that you'll sooner or later come to think you need."[4]

Most states establish specific hunting regulations for bow-and-arrow hunters and for hunters who use muzzle-loaders. The state of Arizona, for example, has three separate seasons for the hunting of pronghorn antelopes: one for general (gun) hunting, one for muzzle-loaders only, and one for bow-and-arrow hunters. The beginning and length of seasons differs somewhat from region to region within the state.

The purpose of age and sex limits is to ensure the survival of game animal populations. Imagine what might happen if hunters killed a large fraction of females and young animals this year. That would mean that fewer animals would be born and fewer would live to be adults next year. Like all game laws, age and sex limits can change from year to year, and they differ from state to state. Until recently, the state of Colorado allowed hunters to kill nursing female bears. The bear population was so large that wildlife managers were not concerned about survival of the species. That situation is different today. Bear populations have declined, and the hunting of nursing female bears is limited in Colorado.

Many states protect female and young deer. In most parts of Montana, for example, a hunter can kill one mule deer or white-tailed deer of either sex during the hunting season. But in some regions, there are also limitations as to the age of mule deer that can be taken. The hunter judges the age of the deer by the number of points on its antlers. Thus, laws distinguish between four-point, two-point, and "spike" (antlerless) deer.

"Bag limits" restrict the number of animals a hunter may kill in one day and in one season. For large game animals, that number is usually small, often no more than a single animal. One purpose of bag limits is to allow many hunters to have a chance to kill an animal.

Some animals are so rare that the concept of bag limits does not apply. In 1990, for example, the state of California decided that it would allow the killing of only six rare Nelson bighorn sheep throughout the state. Permits for hunting the sheep were awarded by a lottery. Everyone who wanted to kill a Nelson bighorn submitted an application. The six lucky hunters were drawn by random from the list of applicants.

NATIONAL HUNTING LAWS

Hunting is permitted in national forests, in some wildlife refuges, and on other federally owned lands. Hunting regulations in these areas are established by federal law and administered by the Department of Agriculture, the Fish and Wildlife Service, the Bureau of Land Management, and other federal agencies responsible for these lands. In general, the kind of hunting restrictions applied to federal lands are similar to those used by state game agencies.

One area of special concern to federal agencies involves migratory birds. A number of species travel from one part of North America to another part—and even beyond—during a single year—for example, snipes, woodcocks, rails, and Canada geese. No single state can regulate the hunting of these birds. In fact, migratory bird hunting laws often involve treaties among the United States, Canada, Mexico, and other nations.

Laws dealing with migratory birds establish specific hunting season and bag limits for each species. For example, federal laws place a limit of three sandhill cranes per day, up to a maximum of six birds. Hunting season dates for the bird differ from one part of the country to another. Federal laws also restrict the type of hunting that can be done. For example, many bird hunters use decoys and bird calls. A decoy is any live or artificial bird that is used to lure game birds to an area. Hunters often place decoys on a pond or a lake to attract birds flying overhead. A bird call is any instrument that a hunter uses to make sounds like those of the bird being hunted. Federal law permits the use of artificial decoys and bird calls in the hunting of migratory birds but does not permit the use of live decoys or tape recordings of bird calls.[5]

Probably the two most important pieces of federal hunting legislation were the Game and Wild Birds Preservation and Disposition Act of 1900 and the Federal Aid in Wildlife Restoration Act of 1937. Both acts are better known by their sponsors' names: the former as the Lacey Act and the latter as the Pittman-Robertson (or P-R) Act.

The Lacey Act dealt with a number of wildlife issues. It banned the shipment of illegally killed birds across state lines. For example, a hunter who illegally killed a sandhill crane in Wyoming could not take the bird across the state line into Colorado. The Lacey Act also placed limitations on the shipment and sale of feathers, skins, and other wildlife products. One motivation for the Act was the widespread destruction of birds to collect feathers and plumes for ladies' hats. The Act placed strict conditions on the transportation of these items. In addition, the Lacey Act regulated the introduction of exotic wildlife into the United States. One animal to which the law was applied was the mongoose. Because it is such an efficient killer of rats, the mongoose had been imported first to the West Indies and then to Hawaii. In both places, however, the mongoose also destroyed a number of other native animals, such as the Hawaiian goose.[6] The Lacey Act prevented the importation of the mongoose to the North American continent, foreseeing the disastrous results that would have followed.

The Lacey Act was significant because it was the first statement of federal wildlife policy. Before its passage, wildlife management had been entirely the responsibility of the states. Also, the Act extended the concept of wildlife management to include more than just hunting seasons and bag limits. It was extended and its enforcement strengthened in amendments of 1976.

The Pittman-Robertson (P-R) Act was an attempt to provide funds to states for improved wildlife management programs. These funds were to come from a 10 percent tax on the sale of sporting guns and ammunition. The tax was later increased to 11 percent and extended to include the sale of handguns.

P-R appropriations are awarded to states for the support of wildlife research, acquisition and development of land, financing of day-to-day wildlife management operations, law enforcement, public relations programs, and hunter safety programs. Funds are allocated to states using a system that counts both the number of hunters in a state and the land area of the state. This system guarantees that large states with small populations (such as Nevada and Montana) will receive their fair share of P-R funds.

P-R legislation requires that states contribute to this program. For every $3 the federal government awards, a state is expected to add $1 of its own money. States are expected to spend *all* of their P-R money on wildlife programs. If they fail to do so, they may be cut off from future P-R funding.

Both the P-R Act and a corresponding act for fishing (the Dingell-Johnston, or D-J, Act) have "profoundly influenced the course of wildlife and fisheries management in the United States."[7] They have made possible a whole range of activities, such as research, that individual states had previously not had the funds or the inclination to carry out.

Hunters are often enthusiastic about the P-R Act. They refer to the contributions they make through the act as evidence of their commitment to conservation programs. In talking about the act, Montana's Fish, Wildlife, and Parks director, K. L. Cool, said that "here in Montana, we're extremely proud of what the American sportsman has done for both game and nongame species."[8] Antihunters are less pleased with the way P-R money is spent. They point out that in 1990, only 13 percent of P-R funds were spent on buying wildlife habitat. About half of the money is spent instead on developing new habitat, such as building ponds and waterholes. Hunting magazines often provide specific examples of the way P-R funds are used to improve game animals and habitat. The August 1991 issue of *Field and Stream,* for example, carried a report of a 7,600-acre parcel of land that will open up new areas for the hunting of deer, elk, cougar, bear, and other animals. The writer points out that the money for this purchase came from the Utah license revenues and federal taxes on sporting goods (i.e., P-R funds).[9]

ENFORCEMENT OF HUNTING LAWS

Hunting laws are in a somewhat different category from most other types of law in our society. A person who runs a red light or robs a bank is likely to be observed in the act. The chances of law enforcement officers' catching these lawbreakers is relatively high. But a person who shoots four birds too many or who kills a protected animal is likely to be miles away from the nearest game warden or even the nearest hunter. Breaking a hunting law is easy, and one's chances of getting caught are small.

Game wardens often find evidence of illegal hunting after a hunter has left the area. They may come across the carcasses of dead animals, or they may encounter hunters who are using illegal equipment. On one occasion, rangers in the Arctic National Park saw an airplane with guns attached to its wings, allowing the pilot to strafe wolves from the air. They knew what the pilot was planning to do, but unless they actually caught him in the act of illegal hunting, they could not stop him.[10] On another occasion, wardens in Yellowstone National Park caught an illegal hunter only because he had accidentally shot himself in the foot after illegally killing ten coyotes.[11]

These examples explain why game wardens have to be clever in tracking down illegal hunters. One technique they sometimes use involves roadblocks in hunting areas to catch hunters who have violated the law. Such roadblocks in Utah and Idaho in 1990 showed that 25 to 40 percent of those stopped were in violation of one or more game laws.[12]

A technique used by federal game agents is to set up undercover operations like those used against drug dealers. In these operations, game wardens try to make friends with other hunters. When the wardens go hunting with their new friends, they watch for violations of game laws.

In 1989, the Fish and Wildlife Service had nine full-time undercover agents, who found out about a number of important illegal hunting operations. In one, falcons were captured and smuggled to Saudi Arabia, where they were sold to royalty. In another, members of a hunting guide service killed black bears for their gallbladders, which were then exported to Japan. In a third case, agents uncovered hunting violations in forty-one of forty-two Texas hunting clubs they visited.[13]

The FWS also has begun to make use of advanced technology in their efforts to locate illegal hunting. In 1990, conservationists, business leaders, hunters, and others chipped in to buy the Service a Bell Jet Ranger helicopter. The helicopter was put to work in Louisiana, where illegal shooting of ducks was beginning to have a continent-wide effect on populations of the birds.[14]

Similar operations are carried on at the state level. Game officials from Connecticut, Massachusetts, and New York worked together until 1989 to arrest 28 people who were charged with 962 violations of game laws.[15]

Because hunting laws are so difficult to enforce, hunter education programs usually stress that hunting laws are not just statements of the way hunters *must* behave. They also describe ethical ways that hunters *should* interact with wildlife. They are designed not primarily as limitations on hunting behav-

A stone-age cave painting of a boar

Queen Elizabeth I enjoyed hunting with her falcons.

A wealthy hunter killing lions
in ancient Assyria

African safaris were commonplace
at one time. Shown here to the left of the
rhino is President Theodore Roosevelt.

Daniel Boone was the most famous American hero who made a reputation by hunting.

Fur trading was once an important industry in North America.

Above: Nineteenth-century North America
was a hunter's paradise.
Below: The passenger pigeon, once so numerous
that flocks of them blotted out the sun,
was hunted to extinction by the early part
of the twentieth century. Not one survives
today, even in a zoo.

Native Americans hunting

American bison—buffalo—
once covered the plains
in North America.

Buffalo were killed
from trains in the
nineteenth century.

Thanks to the efforts of conservationists and various
government agencies, buffalo can still be seen today.
Shown here are buffalo grazing in the National Bison
Range in Montana. Compare the number of buffalo
in this *protected* area with the number shown in the previous
two illustrations, which depict animals in *unprotected* areas.

Above: Natural predators, such as wolves, partially control the size of the population of game animals like deer.

A trophy caribou taken in British Columbia

The Dall sheep is one
of the four animals
in the Grand Slam
of big-game hunting.

Ivory tusks from dead
elephants in Tanzania

A white rhino

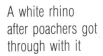

A white rhino
after poachers got
through with it

Skulls of poached
elephants and rhinos

A young hunter with his kill

A hunter with her stone sheep head

A camouflaged bow hunter

White-tailed deer. Deer are the most popular big-game animals with U.S. hunters.

Above: An anti-fur protest

Facing page, top: A trapped animal. *Bottom:* Canada goose killed by lead poisoning from shot.

Protesting a deer hunt in the Everglades organiz
to kill starving deer

ior but as conservation guides for the maintenance of wildlife populations.

Game agencies therefore adopt slogans that encourage compliance with hunting laws, as well as threatening lawbreakers. Examples of such slogans include "Stretch your story, not your bag limit"[16] and "Laws and regulations are designed to protect wildlife and to provide for an equitable distribution of harvestable animals."[17]

Most spokespersons for hunting groups tend to support game laws enthusiastically. In fact, they point out that such laws are often passed as a result of initiatives by hunters. One hunting columnist recommends that young hunters try to win the respect of nonhunters by reminding them of how laws help keep hunting and animal populations in balance.[18]

Hunters are not necessarily completely in accord with the way hunting laws are enforced, however. A 1991 issue of the Wildlife Legislative Fund of America *Update* complained that officers of the Fish and Wildlife Service were too concerned with making arrests for trivial violations, just to record a large number of arrests. The newsletter also criticized the Service's undercover operations, aimed at catching illegal hunters, as "ineffective, wasteful and little more than a publicity stunt."[19]

A number of hunting writers worry that violations of game laws may be the most serious problem hunters face today. Too many hunters exceed bag limits, hunt out of season, or violate other laws either because they do not know the laws well enough, are not well trained in hunting skills, or simply violate the laws intentionally.

Especially troublesome to many hunting groups is the increasing number of so-called slob hunters, hunters whose only aim seems to be to create mayhem in the environment. Joel Scrafford, a senior agent with the Fish and Wildlife Service in Montana, complains that "we see too many four-wheel-drive, assault-rifle, gun-and-run, shoot-anything yahoos who think they're Rambo."[20] An example of this behavior is the report of three young men who killed forty deer in Montana "just for fun."[21]

Many hunters and hunting groups argue for more hunter education classes and perhaps for licensing of all hunters. George Reiger, conservation columnist for *Field and Stream,* warns that "if we lose hunting, it will be because we're too demanding of rights and too indifferent to responsibilities."[22]

Still, a large number of hunters consciously decide not to obey state and national game laws. They kill endangered or protected species and exceed bag limits because of monetary profit or the desire for personal trophies. These people present what may be the most serious threat to wildlife in the world today.

POACHING

As long as there have been game laws, there has been poaching. Poaching is the illegal taking of a protected game animal. During the Middle Ages, poaching represented no threat to the survival of wildlife. Game animals in the king's forests were never threatened by extinction as a result of poaching by peasants. Until quite recently, poaching continued to have virtually no effect on the survival of an animal species. Only in the past few decades has poaching become a major concern of wildlife managers and legitimate hunters.

Today poaching is a major concern in North America, Africa, and Asia. Officials of the National Park Service, for example, regard poaching as the third most serious threat facing U.S. national parks today. In Africa, a number of major game animals are threatened with extinction as a result of poaching.

POACHING FOR PROFIT IN NORTH AMERICA

In 1985, agents of the National Park Service and the Fish and Wildlife Service initiated an antipoaching program called Operation Smoky. The program was designed to find out how much poaching of black bears was going on in the Great Smoky Mountains National Park at the time. They also hoped to catch some of the poachers.

When the operation ended in 1988, the results were both amazing and frightening. Agents had discovered 385 bear claws, 77 feet, 266 gallbladders, 4 heads, 9 hides, and 1 live bear club.[1] In addition, they had uncovered some of the tools poachers use in their trade: electric bone saws, special butcher knives, heavy-duty winches, and oversize refrigerators.

The motivation behind the Great Smoky Mountains poaching was what it nearly always is today: money. Each part of the black bear that agents had found was of special monetary value. Claws were to be used for making jewelry. Feet were to be served as a food, headed perhaps for growing Asian communities around Washington, D.C. Gallbladders were to become a drug, regarded as having unique healing powers by many Asian peoples. Bear heads are valued as trophies. And the bear cub might have been headed for a zoo.

Each part of the bear had its dollar value. And a significant value it was. Dried gallbladder, for example, sells for more than $500 an ounce in Asian pharmacies. Those taken from a national park have even higher value because the bears they come from have not been exposed to the pollution that exists outside the parks.[2] One park ranger described poachers' motives as "pure greed. If they could make money by killing the last bear around," he said, "they wouldn't have hesitated."[3]

The Great Smoky Mountains story is being repeated again and again throughout North America today. One factor behind this trend is a growing Asian population, both in North America and around the world. For many Asians, the meat of wild animals is a special delicacy, creating a new demand on this continent. In addition, Asian healers have long taught about the special curative powers of elk and deer antlers and bear genitals, eyeballs, and gallbladders. Like bear gallbladders, elk antlers may sell for hundreds of dollars an ounce.

A series of raids similar to Operation Smoky was conducted in California in the late 1980s. The purpose of the raids was to break up poaching activities in the state that were producing more than $100 million a year in profits in animal parts. The operation was called Operation Ursus, *ursus* being the Latin word for bear. Ursus was successful, resulting in the arrest of fifty-two poachers and dealers. However, only eighteen months later, other poachers and dealers had taken over the activities of those arrested, and the trade in animal parts was back to normal again.[4]

POACHING AND CULTURAL TRADITIONS

In some cultures, hunting has a long and honored tradition. The killing of an animal means a great deal more than just getting food for the dinner table. Many Native American tribes use animal body parts in ceremonial dances and clothing and in the treatment of illness. Among the Apaches, for example, medicine men use eagle feathers, bones, and claws for the healing of disease. Today, the Apaches cannot kill enough eagles legally to get all of the body parts they need. The Fish and Wildlife Service provides them with the carcasses of as many dead birds as they can. But that is not enough to meet the tribe's needs. The tribe may see poaching as the only solution to its problem. Those who provide poached birds may be either Caucasians or Native Americans. They can earn up to $50 for a single tail feather and $100 for a good wing feather.[5]

POACHING FOR TROPHIES

Big-game hunters are also clients of poachers. Sometimes hunters will simply pay a poacher to kill a prized animal for him or her. Especially in demand today is the Dall sheep. The Dall sheep is one of the four animals considered to be the "Grand Slam" of big-game hunting. The term "Grand Slam" was first suggested by writer Grancel Fitz in a *True* magazine article about 1950. Fitz used the term in talking about how few hunters had been able to kill all four varieties of native North American sheep. The other animals in the Grand Slam are the stone sheep, Rocky Mountain sheep, and desert bighorn. Some hunters will pay $50,000 for the head of a Dall sheep killed by a poacher.

The problem is that many trophy animals are now threatened or endangered. The desire of a hunter to add a highly prized trophy animal to his or her collection comes into conflict with society's efforts to save the animal from extinction.

Capturing trophy hunters who poach has become an important activity of the Fish and Wildlife Service's Division of Law Enforcement. FWS agents have discovered that some of the best-known hunters and wildlife officials in the United States have been involved in poaching. For example, Andrew Samuels is a member of the Safari Club International Hall of Fame and was nominated in 1990 for the Weatherby Award, which goes to the hunter who "collects the greatest number of average as well as record game animals throughout the entire world . . . and [is] a person who has contributed greatly to conservation and hunting education, and one whose character and sportsmanship are beyond reproach."[6] One FWS agent claims that Samuels illegally killed a bighorn sheep in Wyoming as well as more than a half dozen endangered species in other parts of the world. Samuels contests the agent's claims but has agreed to pay $100,000 in fines, spend time in jail, perform eight hundred hours of community service, and give up world hunting for three years.[7]

Big-game poachers often work through supposedly reputable animal organizations to collect their trophies. In September 1990, John Funderburg, formerly curator of the North Carolina Museum of Natural Sciences, pled guilty to charges of unlawfully possessing endangered species.[8] For a number of years, Funderburg had been advising hunters as to how they could kill big game illegally, donate it to the museum, obtain tax credits for their donation, and then, in many cases, get the animals back again.[9]

On occasions, poachers have obtained assistance even from the federal government. In the early 1980s, FWS agents arrested 1986 Weatherby Award winner Thornton Snider for importing endangered species he had killed overseas. Assistant Secretary of the Interior G. Ray Arnett, a friend of Snider's, ordered agents to return Snider's trophy animals to him. The understanding was that Snider would build a museum in which to display the trophies. Although Snider did not build the museum, he apparently did donate the animals to the Los Angeles County Museum of Natural History. The handling of this affair puzzled FWS agents, however. Said one of them, "Giving back an endangered species is about the same as giving back a pound of cocaine."[10]

One concern among conservationists is that scientists still do not know a great deal about the ecology of big-game animals. For example, biologists are not even sure about the size of the population of many game animals. Nor do they understand all of the conditions that may contribute to their survival or extinction. Still, the predicted effects of poaching are frightening. Some biologists believe, for example, that the death of no more than two female grizzlies in Yellowstone National Park may threaten the survival of that whole population of bears.

THE TECHNOLOGY OF POACHING

Poaching is an unsavory business often carried out by unsavory characters. Fish and Wildlife Service officials say that poaching profits are so large that convicted drug and weapons dealers have now been attracted to the business.[11] One poacher convicted in Washington state, for example, had sold 25 eagles for $512,650, 135 elk for $28,500, 286 deer for $24,270, 18 native cats for $15,150, 12 seals for $14,500, and 9 hawks for $2,775.[12]

With this kind of payoff, there is no limit to the means that poachers will use to kill the animals they want. Law enforcement agencies have confiscated everything from crude weapons like hatchets and meat cleavers to sophisticated telemetry devices (for following the movement of animals at a distance), night vision devices, gun silencers, and scanners (to listen in on messages of law enforcement officers).

As an example, Alaskan poachers may use airplanes to help big-game hunters pursue grizzly bears that cannot be hunted legally. A plane will drop the hunter in an area where a grizzly has been sighted. Then the plane will fly at the grizzly, frightening it and chasing it toward the hunter. All the hunter needs to do is to stand there and shoot the grizzly at point-blank range. One FWS agent has accused Carolyn Williams, sometimes referred to as the "Queen of the Dallas Safari Club," of killing a grizzly by this method.

Although the agent did not accompany Ms. Williams on the hunt, he was able to prove that she did not stay on the ground for twenty-four hours prior to shooting the bear, as is required by law. Ms. Williams was fined $5,000 for the offense.[13]

TYPES OF POACHERS

Not all poachers are like those responsible for the horrors discovered in Operation Smoky. To be sure, many are professional criminals. But others are hunters who really do not accept the idea of hunting laws and think they should have the right to kill any game animals they find. What about a poor family in northern Minnesota that finds it difficult to get enough food to eat properly? Is it really wrong for the members of this family to kill an extra deer so that they will have enough food for the winter?

In some parts of the United States, hunters would say no. They think that killing a few animals above and beyond the legal limit will not cause the extinction of a species nor the terrible disruption of an animal community. In many cases, hunters have been taking as many animals as they want—legally or illegally—for many years, and they see no reason to change their habits now.

One Louisiana poacher put the case this way: "My daddy settled us in these parts 50 years ago, and we always hunted there. That island has put a lot of food on the table. So what am I gonna do when they tell me I can't hunt there anymore? *I'm gonna go on huntin' there*—that's what I'm going to do."[14]

THE FIGHT AGAINST POACHING

Game officials and sportsmen have accelerated their fight against poachers. Both groups are looking for ways to reduce the illegal slaughter of animals both in North America and around the world. One approach used by the Fish and Wildlife Service has been to create special teams, like the one used in Operation Smoky. A similar effort, called Operation Trophykill, was created to battle poaching in and around Yellowstone National Park in 1984. The operation was successful. The fifty poachers caught were fined a total of $128,138 and sentenced to a total of fifty-one years in prison.[15]

Most authorities believe that education is the most important solution to the problem of poaching. There will never be enough law enforcement agents to capture all of the illegal hunters, but educational programs may be able to make hunters more understanding of their responsibilities for protecting wildlife. The San Francisco Unified School District, for example, has a program in which inner city students go camping in the wilderness. There they are taught about conservation, including the need to develop respect for life.

Convicted poachers are sometimes used in such educational programs. In 1991, for example, an Eskimo hunter convicted of poaching walruses for their tusks agreed to take part in an educational video about illegal hunting. The video is now used in Alaskan communities to educate both children and adults about the poaching problem.[16]

Hunting agencies in the government and in private hunting groups stress the need for hunters to monitor their own sport. Most states now encourage both hunters and ordinary citizens to look for and report on instances of poaching they learn about. Toll-free numbers have been installed that allow a person to call in and report any poaching that has been seen. State hunting law brochures often remind hunters how important antipoaching campaigns are to their sport.

"It must stop" is one of the slogans that appears on all copies of California hunting restrictions.

Stiff fines and jail sentences are another way to combat poaching. These factors finally convinced many Cajun hunters that their long tradition of taking any amount of any kind of game they wanted any time they wanted was no longer feasible. As one hunter explained, stiffer enforcement of hunting laws "curbed the heck out of poaching. It just wasn't worth going to jail for."[17]

Law enforcement officials are also beginning to use modern technology in their battle against poaching. One problem for FWS agents has always been the difficulty of identifying body parts that were recovered in undercover operations. Now, the Service has a new forensics laboratory that uses advanced scientific techniques to identify animal remains, animal parts, and medicines made out of poached animals. In some cases, blood from a poached animal can be identified on a hunter suspected of the crime.[18]

Still, game officials in North America are making relatively little progress against poaching. In a controlled experiment conducted by wildlife officials in Alberta, only 8 of 752 poaching crimes (just over 1%) were detected.

There are at least three reasons that antipoaching efforts are not always effective. First, for normal, everyday enforcement of game laws, there is just too much space to cover and too few rangers to patrol that space. Antipoaching activities are the responsibility of two hundred special agents from the Fish and Wildlife Service and seven thousand state conservation officers.[19] That number is just too small to monitor the total land areas where poaching occurs.

Second, special operations like Smoky and Trophykill are relatively expensive. New rangers have to be hired and provided with support. In a time of government cutbacks, these additional expenses seldom get funded.

And third, punishment of convicted poachers is sometimes mild. For example, Bruce Loeb, a big-game hunter who poached a grizzly and a caribou in Alaska, was fined $500. Although such crimes can carry a $5,000 fine and a six-month jail sentence, penalties seldom exceed Loeb's fine. U.S. District Court Judge H. Russel Holland explained Loeb's mild sentence. "In my mind," he said, "these offenses are no more serious than a moderate traffic offense, like speeding."[20] That kind of philosophy may be one reason that enforcement efforts against poaching have had such limited success.

POACHING IN AFRICA

A 1990 article on poaching in Africa was entitled "Farewell to Africa." After a six-week tour of the continent, the author was thoroughly discouraged. He felt that there was little to prevent wildlife in Africa from going the way of wildlife in Europe and North America. And the most important factor in the destruction of African game animals was poaching.

Elephants have been the most visible victims of poaching. Their numbers have declined from about 1.3 million in the early 1980s to fewer than 600,000 today. In Kenya alone, 85 percent of the elephant herd has been killed in the past twenty years.[21]

One reason for elephant poaching is the demand for their ivory tusks. The ivory goes primarily to Asia, where it is used for jewelry, statues, and, in Japan, personalized signature stamps. At one point, ivory sold for $120 a pound on the world market. In a single poaching expedition, an African hunter could earn a few hundred dollars. That would be equivalent to the *annual* average income for a resident of Kenya ($290) or Somalia ($228). Under those circumstances, the author of "Farewell to Africa" asks, "Could anyone blame the black East Africans for any of what we'd seen?"[22]

Some progress has been made on this problem. In 1989, the United States, the European Economic Community, and other nations around the world agreed to a worldwide ban on trade in elephant products. Although China, South Africa, Zimbabwe, and Botswana refused to participate in this agreement, the ban has been very successful. In a period of only two years, the price of ivory dropped to less than $3 a pound. The World Wildlife Fund was able to declare that there was "apparently no market for raw ivory right now." Japan, the world's largest consumer of ivory, agreed to the ban. And although China ignored the ban, its markets seemed to have suffered badly anyway. The Beijing Ivory Factory, once one of the largest in the world, was able to keep only 5 ivory carvers out of an original staff of 550.[23]

Profit is not the only motive for poaching. Population has skyrocketed throughout Africa over the past few generations. In Kenya, for example, the population has nearly tripled between 1960 and 1990, from 10 million to about 25 million. That trend will continue well into the twenty-first century.

Growing populations mean, for one thing, the destruction of wildlife habitat. They also mean a more intense search for food. Many species that have little or no economic value are threatened simply for the food they can provide mushrooming populations.

Elephants are not the only threatened species. Less well publicized is the poaching of other animals, such as leopards. In January 1990, for example, government officials in Kenya confiscated thirteen thousand leopard skins from poachers.[24]

As especially attractive target for African poachers is the rhinoceros (both black and white). The rhino's horn is highly prized in Asian cultures as an aphrodisiac, a sexual stimulant. A single horn can bring a poacher more than $10,000. Since the rest of the rhino has no value to the poacher, the animal—minus its horn—is usually left to decay in the forest.

One park ranger in Zimbabwe has described the temptation that rhinos pose for poachers. "Imagine $1–2 million [the equivalent amount when compared to local wages] walking around the streets of the Bronx. How long do you think it would last?"[25] For the rhinoceros, the answer seems to be "not long."

REVERSING THE TREND IN AFRICA

African governments have begun to step up their campaigns against poaching. As in North America, they are exploring a number of different ideas for reducing the illegal killing of their game. In some parts of Africa, wildlife agencies have created new shoot-to-kill teams to use against poachers. The continent's model program is that of Zimbabwe. There, the nation's Parks Department spends more than 30 percent of its budget on antipoaching activities. Its rangers are armed with the most modern weapons. They even have helicopter gunships at their command. As of 1988, government agents had killed 37 poachers and captured 31 more. Chief Warden Glenn Tatham's warning to poachers is that "anyone who comes in armed gets shot at."[26]

In some countries, more desperate measures are being taken. The most intense campaigns are aimed at saving rapidly dwindling populations of black and white rhinos. One approach has been to remove the three hundred remaining black rhinos from their native habitat along the Zambezi River to safer areas within Zimbabwe. And twenty-four-hour armed guards have been placed around the last few dozen white rhinos remaining on the continent.

What may be the most successful method for saving threatened game species is game farms. Game farms are areas of land where desirable game animals are kept, protected, and raised, in much the same way that domestic animals are. The cost of game farming is paid partly by allowing hunters to come onto the game farm and kill a limited number of animals. The philosophy of game farming, then, is to "kill them to save them." That is, by allowing hunters to kill a few game animals, enough money is collected to allow the preservation of whole populations.

Game farming tends to be a successful method because conservation is in the economic best interests of the person who owns the farm. He or she will provide animals on the farm with the best possible care and protection since those animals are the basis of the farm's survival.

Again, Zimbabwe is the model of success for this approach to wildlife conservation. By 1988, five hundred landowners had expressed an interest in opening game farms. Initial studies showed that game farmers were earning 150 to 400 percent as much from their game animals as from domestic cattle. "People will pay a lot of money to see or hunt wildlife," according to one African ecologist.[27]

It is still too early to know how successful game farming and other antipoaching methods will be. Many experts are pessimistic. Zimbabwe park ranger Mark Brightman flatly says about poaching activities, "We're just not winning."[28] The economic incentives for poaching and the problems of catching poachers are so great, authorities say, that it seems hard to believe we will be able to save all wildlife species. Without a dramatic turnaround, the black rhino, white rhino, and other endangered animals may, within our lifetime, be added to the list of species wiped out by humans.

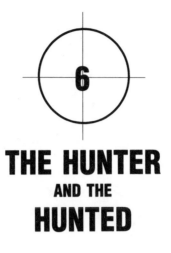

THE HUNTER
AND THE
HUNTED

What does the average hunter in the United States look like? Every five years, the U.S. Fish and Wildlife Service conducts a national survey on the characteristics of hunters, fishermen, and other wildlife enthusiasts, what they do, and how they spend their money. Based on the results of the 1985 survey, one might say that the average hunter in the United States is a white male between the ages of twenty-five and thirty-four, with an annual household income of $30,000 to $50,000, living in a rural area in Illinois, Indiana, Michigan, Ohio, or Wisconsin.

THE HUNTER

In fact, the description of "the average hunter" has only limited value. In 1985, 16.7 million Americans—9 percent of the U.S. population—called themselves hunters. That percentage has slowly been increasing over the years that the Fish and Wildlife Service has been conducting its survey. With that many hunters, one would expect a great variety as to age, income, education, and other traits.

Two features of the "average hunter" description are reasonably accurate, those concerning race and sex. The vast majority of U.S. hunters are white (96%) and male (91%).[1] Any image of hunters as poor or uneducated, however, is incorrect. Nearly half have a high school education, while another 34 percent have had some college education. Just over half earn more than $30,000 a year.

The prevalence of hunters in rural areas (53% of all hunters) is hardly surprising. For one thing, areas for hunting are more accessible in rural than in urban areas. In addition, hunting seems to be more of a cultural and family tradition in rural than in urban areas.

Studies have shown that a majority of hunters grew up in rural areas. They were taught to hunt as a father-to-son tradition. This tradition helps to explain why fewer women become hunters. Only the firstborn or only girl in a hunting family is likely to benefit from the otherwise typical father-to-son tradition.[2] Most hunters (76%) learned to hunt before the age of fifteen and were taught by their father or mother (62%) or by friends of the same age (12%).

Some men feel that hunting is more common among men than women because it involves very special, almost instinctual masculine needs. George Reiger, conservation columnist of *Field and Stream*, argues that all individuals, men and women, must go through a process of initiation that reveals to them "the power of life and death." For women, that process is childbirth. Men do not have a similar, biological process, so throughout history, Reiger believes, "boys have intuitively sought passage into manhood through enduring some ritual of hardship or suffering." In modern society, Reiger says, hunting may provide that act of initiation for boys. The sport "enables a boy to seek and find manhood without the attendant guilt of killing other humans."[3]

The nation's 16.7 million hunters spent a total of 34 million days with their sport in 1985. That time was divided almost equally between big-game hunting (132.3 million days) and small-game hunting (131.3 million days). Hunters also spent 41.7 million days hunting migratory birds and 47.1 million days hunting other animals, such as coyotes, crows, foxes, groundhogs, prairie dogs, and raccoons. These animals are sometimes classified as "varmints," or pests.

The average hunter spent $614 on his or her sport in 1985. About a third of that went for equipment (guns, bows and arrows, decoys, ammunition, etc.), a third for trip-related expenses, such as food, lodging, transportation, guide fees, and licenses, and a third on other expenses, such as magazines, membership dues, contributions, and land leasing. An increasing fraction of a hunter's costs go to the leasing of private land, fees for the use of such land, or membership in private clubs that own hunting lands.

Hunting is also popular among youths aged six through fifteen. In 1985, 1.8 million boys and girls (5% of the U.S. population for this age group) were hunters. As with older age groups, many of these young hunters also participated in fishing as a recreational activity. The characteristics of young hunters tended to be much like those of older hunters. They were most likely to be male (90%) and white (95%) and from a middle-class home in a rural area. The only difference in these characteristics is that young hunters are more likely to come from the west south central states (Arkansas, Louisiana, Oklahoma, and Texas) than from any other part of the nation.

WHY HUNTERS HUNT

Why hunt? Until the past few decades, that question would have seemed absurd to most hunters. Killing game for food or for sport has, for most of human history, seemed entirely normal and natural. Lately, however, more and more hunters seem to feel that they must defend their sport. Thus, over the past decade, both sporting and general interest magazines have carried a number of "Why I Hunt" articles.

All of the hunting arguments offered, however, tend to fall into a rather small number of categories. Those categories were investigated and described in a large study on attitudes toward wildlife, conducted in the 1970s by Professor Stephen Kellert of Yale University.[4]

Kellert identified the nine attitudes toward wildlife listed in Table 2. The vast majority of hunters fell into one of three of these categories: utilitarian, dominionistic, and naturalistic. Many hunters held attitudes in more than one of these categories.

Utilitarian hunters have also been described as "meat hunters." They view hunting as a way of get-

TABLE 2

ATTITUDES OF AMERICANS TOWARD WILDLIFE

Category	Characteristics
Utilitarian	Practicality; usefulness
Dominionistic	Mastery; superiority
Naturalistic	Wildlife exposure; contact with nature
Ecologistic	Ecosystems; interdependence of species
Humanistic	Love for animals; pets
Moralistic	Ethical concern for animal welfare
Scientific	Study of animals
Aesthetic	Artistic interest
Negativistic	Avoidance, dislike, fear

From Stephen R. Kellert, *A Study of American Attitudes toward Animals,* Washington, D.C.: U.S. Fish and Wildlife Service, 1976.

ting food, skins, and other animal products for human use. They are not especially interested in the beauty of nature or the social contact with others that hunting provides. Roughly four in ten (44%) of the hunters surveyed by Kellert fell into this category. Dan Sisson, a columnist for *Field and Stream* magazine, explains one of the reasons that he hunts. "I hunt for food," he says, "and I do not choose to delegate my right to obtain it to a slaughterhouse. My friends go to supermarkets and buy packaged beef and lamb. I go into the wilderness and kill elk, venison, and wildfowl."[5]

For about a third (38%) of Kellert's subjects, hunting was viewed as a contest between hunter and prey. These hunters regard their sport as not so different from football or other forms of competitive athletics. These "dominionistic" or "sport" hunters had little interest in or emotional feelings for animals. For them, game animals were trophies to be won in combat.

Trophy hunters often like to save a particular portion of the animals they kill as souvenirs of the hunt. Animal heads mounted on the wall, elephant feet used as umbrella stands, rugs made of tiger skins, and ashtrays made of bear feet are typical of these trophies. The most successful trophy hunters may set aside entire rooms to display their trophies. Maurice Stans, secretary of commerce under President Richard Nixon, established the Stans Africa Hall in Rock Hill, South Carolina. There he displayed more than ninety animals that he and other trophy hunters had killed during more than ten African safaris.[6] Cleveland Amory claims that there are "hundreds, if not thousands" of these rooms located throughout North America.[7]

The Boone and Crockett Club has developed a rating system that gives points for various types of trophy animals killed. These points are based on various measurements of an animal, such as weight, height, and length of antlers or tusks. Each year, a list of the most valuable trophy animals killed, based on the point system, is published. Many hunters tell of their excitement in killing an animal that will qualify for the trophy list. One woman describes her experience as one of the eight hunters in California in 1990 allowed to hunt a desert bighorn sheep: "I took a deep breath, let it out, and shot. The ram fell in a heap. I yelled. Bill yelled, and we hugged. I skimmed the mountaintop, barely hearing Bill's warning to be careful, and I got to the ram first. He was gorgeous! . . . My Boone and Crockett Club score was $16\frac{2}{8}$. . . . I was so proud!"

Sport hunters often talk about this kind of pride. A Michigan hunter searched for an explanation for why he loved hunting. Eventually he decided that it was a sense of accomplishment. "A man needs something to give him pride. Hunting can do that for you," he said.[8]

"Naturalistic" hunters made up only 18 percent of those in the Kellert study, but they were also the ones who hunted most frequently. For naturalistic hunters, returning to a simpler, more natural way of life is important. Hunting is an important way of escaping from the pressures of everyday life.

President George Bush is a typical naturalistic hunter. He explained his feelings about the sport this way: "It's the excitement factor, the outdoors, the love of nature, the beauty that's normally associated with it, the relaxation, the camaraderie. All these things come together."[9] Naturalistic hunters often get passionate about their love of nature. A booklet on hunting and fishing published by the University of Arizona quotes one hunter as saying that hunting "makes me almost religious when I'm sitting on a mountain waiting for a deer sometimes. I almost feel like praying."[10]

Knowing the answer to "why hunt?" is especially important to wildlife managers. Since one of their major responsibilities is to keep hunters satisfied, it is hardly surprising to learn that many studies have been conducted to find out what makes a hunter happy.

If you ask hunters what it takes to satisfy them, you get one type of answer. Most often hunters mention the chance to be out of doors, close to nature. One hunter describes the feeling this way: "I've got a favorite place on the rim of a large canyon in northern Utah where I like to just sit and stare out over a vast chunk of wild, spectacular country, especially after things have begun to settle down after the opening week melee."[11]

But if you compare groups of hunters who say they are satisfied with their hunting with those who are dissatisfied, you get a different response. In this case, what matters most is that a hunter has killed an animal or shot at an animal or, at the very least, seen an animal. So, based on deeds and not words, the satisfied hunter is not so much one who gets back to nature but one who has a chance to see and shoot at animals.[12]

Sometimes it appears that the *only* thing that makes a difference to some hunters is the chance to kill an animal. Three people in Monterey County, California, were arrested in April 1991 for allowing hunters to kill trophy animals while the animals were still in cages. The two men and a woman purchased old animals from zoos and then made them available to hunters for killing. They took the animals into a secluded area in large trailers and then opened the trailer doors to allow the animals out. Since many of the animals had become dependent on humans, some never left the trailer at all. Hunters shot them while they were inside the trailer. Those that left the trailer were all killed within one hundred feet of their cages. The dead animals were then dragged some distance from the trailer, where hunters had their pictures taken with their trophies. Hunters paid $3,000 to $10,000 for the opportunity of killing a trophy animal.[13]

In his book *The Hunt,* John Mitchell talks of interviewing a hunter who had just returned home after opening day of hunting season. He asked the man where he had hunted. The man's reply was "I don't remember. I slept in the back seat going and coming and *where* we was didn't seem to matter when we got there." All he remembered from the whole day of hunting was seeing the white tail of a deer running from him.[14]

Another important factor in hunter satisfaction is the social aspect. Hunters like to pursue their sport together. One study showed that three-fourths of a group of hunters preferred hunting with friends in an area where the chance of killing a deer was 10 percent compared to hunting alone in an area where the chance was 50 percent.[15] One hunter has described the social aspect of hunting. "A hunting partnership is a special thing," he writes. "Months, even years, evaporate as hunting partners reunite at a familiar duck blind or hay field. Partnerships derive their vitality from the sharing. Cold days, looking for lost dogs, miles of brush-busting and campfires are certainly part of it. But the sharing is of kindred attitudes too."[16]

Even when the thrill of killing itself has diminished, many hunters still return to the field because of the chance to be with other hunters. One hunter described this feeling to John Mitchell. He explained how disappointed he was when he did not kill a deer on opening day. But, he explained, it was no longer so important to get a deer. "The real thing," he said, "is the tradition. The hunt. It's something you just have to do every year."[17]

TOOLS OF THE HUNT

In the fourteenth century, guns began to replace the bow and arrow as the most popular hunting weapon. Over the next six hundred years, gun makers invented and developed a wide variety of rifles, shotguns, and pistols for use in the hunt. Indeed, one hunting authority has observed that the needs of hunters were a more important factor in the development of new weapons than were the needs of soldiers.[18]

Today, guns are still the weapons of choice among American hunters. Virtually any type of gun can be and has been used for hunting. This fact constitutes one argument used by the National Rifle Association against gun legislation. Laws that prohibit citizens from owning *any* type of gun are unfair to hunters, the National Rifle Associations says. Even so-called assault weapons can be used in hunting, so attempts to reduce gun-related violence by banning semiautomatic weapons are also seen as an attack on the right of hunters to use the weapon of their choice.[19]

The 1985 Fish and Wildlife Service survey confirms that at least some hunters use just about every type of weapon made, from eighteenth-century muzzle-loaders to modern semiautomatic pistols to bows and arrows. Table 3 shows the amount spent by hunters on various types of weapons in 1985. Rifles and shotguns are the most commonly purchased weapons, with archery equipment not far behind in popularity. Primitive firearms such as muzzle-loaders are still the choice of a relatively small fraction of hunters. In many states, hunting laws provide sepa-

TABLE 3			
EXPENDITURES BY U.S. HUNTERS IN 1985			
	Total Spent (in thousands of dollars)	**Number of Hunters (in thousands)**	**Average Spent per Hunter (in dollars)**
Guns and rifles	$1,312,456	3,507	$374
Rifles	$544,948	1,817	$300
Shotguns	$497,209	1,704	$292
Primitive firearms	$57,227	286	$200
Handguns	$213,073	677	$315
Bows, arrows, other archery equipment	$196,740	1,542	$128

Source: U.S. Department of the Interior, Fish and Wildlife Service, *1985 National Survey of Fishing, Hunting, and Wildlife Associated Recreation,* (Washington, D.C.: U.S. Department of the Interior, 1988), Table 25.

rate hunting seasons for each type of weapon: modern firearms, bow and arrow, and primitive firearms.

Today's hunters have the most sophisticated modern technology at their disposal. Nowhere is this more obvious than in Alaska, where hunters commonly use snowmobiles and airplanes to chase wolves to exhaustion. When the animals are too tired to move, the hunters dismount from their snowmobiles or land their planes to shoot them, often at point-blank range. Between 1984 and 1987, aerial hunters accounted for 42 percent of all wolves reported killed in Alaska.[20]

State and federal laws prohibit the killing or harassing of animals from the air. They specify that one can use an airplane to chase game animals, but the hunter must get out of the plane before shooting the animal. Therefore, as one author has observed, hunters who use this technique have "fractured the laws." But their attitude seems to be "Who's to see you?"[21]

Furthermore, the Alaska Board of Game has thus far refused to do anything to stop the practice. One hunter defended the use of airplanes by explaining that such technology simply made humans a "superior predator." He claims that he is no more than a "mechanical hawk."[22]

TRAPPING

Another form of hunting is trapping. Trapping is any form of hunting in which an animal is captured and killed or captured and held until recovered by the trapper.

In general, three types of traps are in use. The *leg-hold trap* grabs an animal by the leg when it steps on a release bar. The animal, unless it manages to tear loose, is held by the trap until released by the trapper. The *snare* consists of a wire loop that catches an animal by the neck or the foot. Again, the animal is captured live by the trapper unless it escapes. The *killing trap* contains a metal bar that, when activated, strikes an animal on the head or neck. In most cases, the animal is killed by the trap.

In 1985, 508,000 Americans said that they engaged in trapping for sport (62%) or as a business (32%). Those who trap as a business sell the pelts of the animals they capture, such as muskrat, mink, fisher, marten, fox, otter, red squirrel, and beaver, to the fur industry, where the pelts are made into coats, stoles, and other garments and accessories.

Sixty-two thousand (12%) of all trappers were under the age of sixteen. These youngsters spent an average of seventeen days trapping. The 447,000 trappers over the age of sixteen spent an average of twenty-three days per year on their sport or business.[23]

Even more than hunting, trapping has become

the center of great controversy in North America. Critics complain that traps cause undue suffering of animals and that the wrong animals are sometimes taken in a trap. When a killer trap is used, this error results in the unnecessary death of an unintended victim. Trapping is also criticized as an immoral method of providing humans with luxuries (such as fur coats) that they easily can do without.

THE HUNTED

Which animals do hunters regard as "fair game"? A simpler question to ask might be which animals are *not* hunted. Throughout history, just about every species of wildlife has been regarded as fair game by at least some hunters. Today's hunting magazines include articles on almost every conceivable game animal. Some examples are stories such as "Hare Bawls," "50 Hints for Honkers" (geese), "Climb Every Mountain" (mountain quail), "H_2Onkers" (geese), "Six Methods for Mule Deer," "Cotton up to Rabbits," "Plan Now for Elk Later," "Lower 48 Moose," and "Golden Gobblers" (turkeys).

Traditionally, game animals have been divided into big game, small game, and other animals. Today, migratory birds make up a fourth category.

The animals that belong in each category depend on the location. In Africa, elephants and rhinoceroses are examples of big game. In North America, the term big game usually refers to antelope, bear, deer, elk, moose, and wild turkey. Other types of big game exist—the four Grand Slam trophy sheep, for example—but are less common.

Small game in North America includes grouse, partridge, quail, rabbits, squirrels, and other small birds and animals. The category of "other animals" includes varmints. The migratory birds are those that fly from one part of the world to another during a single year.

Table 4 shows the number of hunters who say they hunt each type of animal in the United States. By far the most popular animal, according to hunters themselves, is the deer. Nearly 12 million men and women say they hunt deer. Wild turkey are the target of nearly 2 million hunters.

The next most popular game animals are small game: rabbits and hares, squirrels, quail, pheasant, grouse, and prairie chicken. Overall, nearly 11 million hunters set their sights on these animals.

Doves, ducks, and geese are the most popular migratory bird targets. About 5 million hunters favor these animals as their prey. Finally, the smallest number of hunters choose "other" animals as their game. But these hunters spend about twice as much time hunting as do big- and small-game and migratory-bird hunters.

The number of animals actually killed by licensed hunters in the United States is somewhat different from the pattern shown in Table 4. As you can imagine, it is easier in most parts of the nation to find and kill a squirrel than it is to find and kill a deer. Table 5 shows the best estimate available of animals taken by U.S. hunters in the 1988–89 season.

Overall, hunters killed just over 100 million birds and about 50 million rabbits and squirrels. By far the main target among big-game hunters were white-tailed deer in the East and mule deer in the West. The kill of other animals, such as bighorn sheep, mountain lion, bison, and wolverine, is due largely to the fact that the population of these animals is quite small.

Table 5 illustrates the impact that hunters have on the environment. In a single year, U.S. hunters killed about 175 million birds and other animals. Similar data are not available for other parts of the

TABLE 4

ANIMALS HUNTED IN THE UNITED STATES, 1985

Animal Hunted	Number of Hunters (in thousands)	Total Hunting Days (in thousands)
BIG GAME		
Deer	11,978	118,768
Wild turkey	1,939	14,862
Elk	776	5,298
Bear	476	4,390
Antelope	228	872
Moose	73	560
Other	303	3,665
SMALL GAME		
Rabbits and hares	6,458	69,436
Squirrels	5,792	61,094
Pheasant	3,652	30,301
Quail	3,162	29,740
Grouse/prairie chicken	2,190	21,489
Other	517	5,232
MIGRATORY BIRDS		
Doves	3,057	19,256
Ducks	2,509	22,314
Geese	1,463	13,128
Woodcock	514	3,419
Coots, rails, gallinules	123	1,593
Other	162	1,094
OTHER ANIMALS		
Raccoon	1,000	20,804
Groundhog (woodchuck)	971	13,376
Coyote	773	9,979
Fox	514	7,617
Crows	451	5,625
Prairie dog	197	2,450
Other	254	3,167

Source: U.S. Department of the Interior, Fish and Wildlife Service, *1985 National Survey of Fishing, Hunting, and Wildlife Associated Recreation,* 1988, Table 10.

TABLE 5

NUMBER OF ANIMALS KILLED IN THE UNITED STATES, 1988–89

Animal	Number Killed
MAMMALS	
Rabbit	25,000,000
Squirrel	22,000,000
White-tailed deer	4,000,000
Mule deer	600,000
Wild turkey	350,000
Coyote	250,000
Pronghorn antelope	115,000
Elk	102,000
Black bear	21,000
Caribou	21,000
Moose	12,000
Javelina	10,000
Bighorn sheep	2,400
Mountain lion	1,500
Mountain goat	1,200
Brown/grizzly bear	1,100
Wolf	1,000
Bison	750
Wolverine	700
Musk ox	90
BIRDS	
Mourning dove	50,000,000
Quail	28,000,000
Pheasant	20,000,000
Ruffed grouse	6,000,000
Duck	5,200,000
Goose	1,300,000
Chukar partridge	1,000,000

Source: Fish and Wildlife Service and the Fund for Animals, cited in Michael Satchell, "The American Hunter under Fire," *U.S. News & World Report,* February 5, 1990, 33.

world. But the effect of hunting on parts of Africa, for example, has been described above.

Humans are certainly the most efficient predators of the animal world today. But is that good or bad? Is hunting a sport to be admired and encouraged, or is it increasingly a remnant of humankind's more primitive history? On that issue, people are in serious disagreement today.

THE CASE
AGAINST HUNTING . . .
AND
HOW HUNTERS RESPOND

Hunters are under attack today. More and more people and organizations are speaking out against the
sport. Magazine and newspaper writers point out reasons to oppose hunting. Concerned citizens lobby for
laws to limit or ban hunting. Animal welfare groups
work through the courts to restrict or abolish hunting
seasons. Those opposed to hunting raise moral and
ethical arguments, point to the threat of hunting to
wildlife, remind us of the dangers to innocent bystanders, and complain about the unnecessary pain
and suffering among animals that hunting can cause.

Hunters are increasingly driven to respond to
these criticisms and to defend their sport. The debate
between the two sides is often bitter and sometimes
violent. Both antihunters and hunters believe in their
philosophies with a passion. For many hunters, their
sport is "one of the ultimate sensual experiences a
human being can experience. Your instincts are involved, your emotions are involved, your senses are
involved. . . . If hunting is in your blood, it's with
you for your whole life." [1]

Antihunters have a very different view of the

sport. In a widely debated article in *Esquire* magazine, writer Joy Williams called American hunters "blood-thirsty, piggish, and grossly incompetent." Animal rights activist Cleveland Amory has proposed the formation of a Hunt-the-Hunters Hunt Club, whose motto would be "If you can't play a sport, shoot one."

THE MORAL ARGUMENTS AGAINST HUNTING . . .

One argument against hunting is a moral one, based on the idea that all forms of life deserve respect. Killing another animal, according to this philosophy, is immoral. Albert Schweitzer taught that "ethics deals not only with people, but also with creatures. . . . The thoughtful cannot help recognizing that kindly conduct toward nonhuman life is a natural requirement of ethics." With regard to hunting, he said that "we must reach the stage at which killing for sport will be felt as a disgrace to our civilization."[2]

Some spokespersons for this viewpoint have used strong, combative language. In a famous 1957 essay on hunting, the naturalist Joseph Wood Krutch called the sport "the perfect type of pure evil for which metaphysicians [that is, philosophers] have sometimes sought." His now widely quoted conclusion was that "when a man wantonly destroys one of the works of man we call him a vandal. When he wantonly destroys one of the works of God we call him Sportsman."[3]

Modern critics are no kinder to hunters. Perhaps the best-known spokesman for the antihunting argument today is Cleveland Amory, founder and president of the Fund for Animals. In a recent article, he argued that hunters are "bloodthirsty nuts." "Hunting is an antiquated expression of macho self-aggrandizement, with no place in a civilized society," he said.[4]

As for the ethics of hunting, Joy Williams claimed that the chief attraction of the sport is purely and simply "the pursuit and murder of animals."[5]

In one of the most powerful statements against hunting, a former hunter has criticized many of the reasons that hunters give for taking part in their sport. When all of those reasons have been analyzed—and rejected—he says, "the naked brutality of hunting defines itself: killing for the fun of it." It was the recognition of this fact, the writer claims, that made him finally realize that hunting was not for him.[6]

Some of the most vocal critics of hunting belong to animal rights groups. These groups believe that humans are not superior to other animals. They say that all species have equal value. As a result, animal activists tend to oppose the wearing of furs and leathers, the eating of meat, and the use of animals for medical research. They say these activities all involve pain, suffering, and cruelty for animals. Ingrid Newkirk, the founder of People for Ethical Treatment of Animals, has put the philosophy this way: "A rat is a pig is a dog is a boy." You should never do anything to an animal that you would consider immoral to do to a human. For animal rights activists, hunting is only one aspect of a more general fight against the cruelty to animals they see in many different human activities.

. . . AND HOW HUNTERS RESPOND

Hunters respond to these arguments by pointing out that the moral issues involved are not clear-cut. The fundamental point is that killing is a fact of life. The law of nature is to kill or be killed, eat or be eaten. "Every living creature takes life to stay alive, and if it doesn't, it quickly starves and dies a slow, agonizing death," says one writer.[7] Hunting is probably "rooted in an innate human interest in predator–prey relationships, an interest very likely tied to the survival value of eating while avoiding being eaten," suggests another writer.[8]

After all, hunters point out, *all* humans eat food that has been killed, if not by themselves, then by someone else. Does the fact that you didn't see the killing take place make it any more or less "moral"? Indeed, hunters may be more moral because they take direct responsibility for the food they eat. They experience firsthand what it feels like to obtain the food one needs. One writer describing only her second hunting experience summarized the feeling this way: "Part of what makes hunting such an intensely emotional experience is the physical responsibility you take for the death of your food."[9]

In fact, most people see a big difference between people who hunt to obtain food and those who hunt only for sport. Professor Kellert's study on hunting attitudes found that 80 percent of Americans approve of hunting as a way of obtaining food. At the same time, 80 percent oppose hunting purely as a sport.

Hunters are especially critical of the arguments used by animal rights activists. They simply do not believe that all animals are equal in value. In reaction to this philosophy, hunters have formed a new organization, Putting People First, which attempts to combat the work of animal rights groups. The organization is not antianimal, one spokesperson points out, but prohuman. It "promotes the age-old view that human rights are above animal rights."[10]

Finally, hunters point out that critics of hunting are not always consistent. For example, Albert Schweitzer himself was not absolutely opposed to hunting. He owned a gun, which he used to kill snakes and predatory birds.[11]

"HUNTERS CAUSE ANIMALS TO SUFFER . . ."

A second complaint of antihunters is that game animals are too often wounded but not killed. These animals are left to wander away and suffer until they die a few hours or days later. Bow-and-arrow hunters seem to be especially vulnerable to this criticism. This weapon is much less efficient at killing than are guns.

Research over a fifteen-year period in Texas found that only half of the deer hit by arrows are killed. The other 50 percent die what must be a slow, painful death. In comparison, 90 percent of all deer shot by guns are killed almost instantly.[12]

Cleveland Amory points out the growing significance of this problem. More traditional weapons like muzzle-loaders and archery equipment are growing in popularity among hunters, but these weapons often do not kill an animal with a single shot. Instead, they tend to cause fatal injuries rather than instant death.[13] As a consequence, we are seeing more crippled and orphaned wildlife.

A second, unintended cause of wildlife injury is the use of lead shot. When animals are hit with lead bullets but not killed, they may absorb some lead into their bodies. Many more animals ingest lead shot while they are feeding. The lead causes toxic effects and, in many cases, death. By one estimate, lead poisoning each year is responsible for the death of 2 to 3 million waterfowl, as well as that of dozens of bald eagles.[14]

Wildlife injuries are a major matter of concern for many nonhunters. Studies have shown that the slow, painful death of wounded animals is the most important objection nonhunters have to the sport. One public survey firm concluded that "the public is revolted by the perceived suffering of hunted wildlife."[15] Of the five most important problems about

101

hunting identified by the respondents to this survey, three dealt with animal suffering: "Wounded animals die a slow death," "Wounded animals die a painful death," and "Leaving a wounded animal to die is sadistic."[16]

. . . AND HOW HUNTERS RESPOND

Hunters recognize that wounded animals are a problem in their sport. No one can expect that every hunter will always kill every animal with the first shot of a gun or bow and arrow. Wounded animals are a fact of life in hunting. Their solution to this problem is to improve their skills as hunters so as to reduce the number of wounded animals and to improve their sensibilities about the suffering of wounded wildlife.

All major hunting groups are actively involved in hunter education programs that include these objectives. For example, the National Rifle Association has a Hunting and Outdoor Skills program in which boys and girls are confronted with the issue of wounded animals. They are reminded that hunters have a responsibility to locate and retrieve wounded game and not to leave them in the field to suffer.[17] The Safari Club International and Wildlife Legislative Fund of America offer similar programs for hunters of all ages.

Hunters are also conscious of the problem of using lead shot. Many are beginning to switch over to steel shot. But others are still reluctant to use steel because it is more expensive and may cause damage to the guns they use, they say.

"HUNTING THREATENS ANIMAL POPULATIONS . . ."

Another argument against hunting is that it threatens the survival of some species. Many people acknowledge that wildlife management has been successful with regard to a few popular game animals. Largely through the efforts of hunting groups, there are now twenty-five times as many elk and forty times as many pronghorn antelopes as there were in 1910.[18] Other animals have not fared as well. Black bear, mountain lion, and bighorn sheep are among the species that many observers feel may be doomed to extinction by hunting. One authority suggests that the 1990s may be a "pivotal juncture for saving our wild animals."[19]

The signs are not very promising. Even though the length of hunting seasons and bag limits have been reduced, for example, the number of migratory birds decreased by 30 percent from the 1970s to the 1980s. In addition, the breeding population of nine of ten duck species decreased in 1989.[20] Some experts believe that hunting is responsible for these changes.

Critics say that a major problem is that wildlife management today is in the hands of hunters. These managers are concerned about the fate of a relatively small number of game species. When pressured, they tend to cave in to demands for increased amounts of hunting time. The practice of having hunters in the position of wildlife managers, according to one critic, is "like having Dracula guard the blood bank."[21]

. . . AND HOW HUNTERS RESPOND

Hunters remind their critics that nature is not as simple as they tend to picture it. Humans are also a part of nature and have been disrupting the environment for thousands of years. It is idealistic and foolish to imagine that a ban on hunting would make life any better for animals.

Dr. Walter Howard, a former biology professor at the University of California at Davis, has outlined this view. "People must assist nature in environments that have been modified by people," he states. If hunters are prevented from killing surplus animals, then animal populations will begin to "self-limit" themselves. And the means of self-limitation—"starvation, cruel diseases, cannibalism, territorial battles, and nest abandonment"—are the very situations we find most unpleasant, according to Dr. Howard.[22]

Besides, hunters point out, most species are threatened not by hunting but by other factors. Among the most important of these are poaching and loss of wildlife habitat. Even if a ban on all hunting were enacted, many wild animals would still be threatened by these forces, they say.

"HUNTERS INJURE AND KILL PEOPLE . . ."

Those opposed to hunting also point to the number of accidental human deaths and injuries it causes each year. In 1988, for example, hunters accidentally killed 177 people and injured 1,719 more.[23]

Many of the dead and injured were hunters themselves. For example, a Long Island man died in 1988 when his shotgun went off while he was using it to club a wounded deer to death.[24] But many hunting victims are innocent bystanders. In a nationally famous case in 1988, a Maine woman was shot to death in her own backyard when a hunter mistook her white mittens for the tail of a deer. The local newspaper criticized the woman for not wearing blaze-orange while she was hanging up her washing, and the local grand jury refused to indict the hunter.[25] Incidents such as these always score public relations points for the antihunting cause.

. . . AND HOW HUNTERS RESPOND

Hunters acknowledge that accidents, like wounded animals, are a part of their sport. They point out that guns and bows and arrows are deadly weapons and that some accidents are inevitable in hunting. But they argue that critics have exaggerated the seriousness of hunting accidents. They say that newspapers and the general public seem to be overly fascinated with gory stories about hunting accidents. John Mitchell points out that the number of hunting deaths in Michigan averaged about fifteen a year during the 1970s. That rate, he reminds the reader, was less than the death rate from drowning for the *total* population and certainly much less than the death rate from drowning among fishermen. He believes that hunting accidents would be much less interesting to the general public if there were more of them.[26]

Still, hunters agree that every effort should be made to reduce the number of hunting accidents. That is another objective of hunter education programs sponsored by groups such as the National Rifle Association, Safari Club International, and the Wildlife Legislative Fund of America. For example, the National Rifle Associations' training manual for young hunters tells readers that "out of concern and respect for human life, your primary responsibility as a hunter is safety. . . . You're also responsible for the safety of anyone within the range of your firearm, including hunting partners, farmers, hikers, cross-country skiers and everyone else who enjoys the outdoors."[27]

TAKING ACTION AGAINST HUNTING

Some antihunters now feel that educational campaigns to ban or limit hunting have not been very effective. They have begun to look for more aggressive methods for taking action against hunters. The two most common forms of actions are harassment of hunters in the field and legal action against hunting.

HUNTER HARASSMENT . . .

Antihunters have invented a variety of activities designed to interfere with hunters. Antihunters have, in one place or another, taken the following steps:

Tried to convince landowners to close their property to hunting.
Played tapes of wolf sounds in the woods, to scare away game animals.
Covered the floors of hunting blinds with manure, rotten eggs, or other smelly materials.
Spread deer repellent in hunting areas.
Worked for legislation that would ban guns in a town or county.

Scared off animals with air horns.
Followed hunters into the woods to try to talk them into giving up their sport.
Applied for scarce hunting permits for rare game, limiting the number of permits that hunters themselves can receive.
Released duck decoys with lighted flares to scare away waterfowl.[1]

Guidelines for hunter harassment have been published by Friends of Animals. The brochure tells antihunters that "angry hunters do not stalk quietly. Disrupt!"[2]

In some cases, antihunters have used extreme measures to discourage hunters. In the 1989 buffalo hunt near Yellowstone National Park, one woman smeared the blood of a dead buffalo on a hunter. She screamed at him that she hoped the buffalo's spirit would haunt him forever.[3] In other cases, antihunters have attacked hunters with all types of weapons and chained themselves to the gates of hunting preserves. They have also been accused of setting traps and putting out poisoned food for hunting dogs.[4]

. . . AND HOW HUNTERS RESPOND

Hunting magazines and organizations have reacted strongly to hunter harassment. They encourage their readers and members to remain calm in the face of antihunter attacks. They remind hunters that confrontations that make the evening news are exactly what antihunters most hope for. A typical suggestion is that hunters make out an information card to take with them when they go hunting. They can hand this information card to any antihunters they may encounter. One piece of information on the card should be that the hunter will be driving game toward other hunters. If antihunters choose to follow a hunter into the field, they will also be participating in a game drive. In some states, to do so without a hunting license is illegal, and antihunters may be arrested and prosecuted.

Some public and private organizations have made special arrangements to keep antihunters from interfering with a hunt. In 1989, for example, Yale University learned that a group of antihunters were planing to interfere with hunters on land the university owned. It decided to require a special permit of anyone hunting on the land. Anyone who did not have a permit—and this included all antihunters—were arrested for trespassing. Similarly, officials at the Great Swamp National Wildlife Refuge in New Jersey have issued special hunting permits since antihunters disrupted a hunt there in 1977. The refuge is closed to anyone who does not have such a permit.[5]

On another front, hunting groups are working to have antiharassment laws passed in all fifty states and on the national level. As of late 1991, forty-four states had already adopted antiharassment laws.[6] In general, these laws make it illegal for someone to interfere with a hunter while he or she is in the field. In some cases, hunters are also allowed to bring civil suits against people who harass them. An example of these laws is that of Maryland. In 1990, eleven antihunters were arrested under the provisions of this law because they interfered with a legal hunt. Nine of the antihunters were fined $500 each, and were two were fined $100 each. One antihunter who refused to pay her fine was sentenced to a fifteen-day jail term instead.[7]

The constitutional status of these laws is not, however, clear. Antihunters claim that most harassment techniques simply involve the exercise of free speech. Laws that limit this right of free speech are therefore unconstitutional, they argue. In 1987, the Connecticut Supreme Court agreed with this argument. It invalidated that state's antiharassment law as being an infringement on antihunters' freedom of speech. Since then a new, more limited revision of the law has been proposed in the state legislature. With pressure from hunting groups to extend antiharassment laws to all states, this debate is likely to continue for a long time to come.

LEGAL ACTION AGAINST HUNTING . . .

People opposed to hunting are also finding a variety of legal maneuvers by which to achieve their ends. They have been most successful thus far in California. In 1989, a coalition of antihunting groups sued the California State Department of Fish and Game (DFG), asking the courts to halt the state's annual bear-hunting season. They claimed that the DFG lacked accurate information about bear populations in the state to specify the number of bear licenses to issue.

The courts agreed with the antihunting groups. Superior Court Justice Cecily Bond ruled that the DFG had to reassess its bear-hunting regulations every year. Until it did so, no bear-hunting season could be held.

The ruling was significant because it applied to *all* species, not just bears. It required the DFG to prepare population reports on all game animals for which it was responsible.

With severe economic conditions in the state, the DFG was placed in a difficult situation. It had to spend more time and money counting bears. As a result of the court action, there was no bear-hunting season in California in 1989 and no bow hunting season in the state in 1990.[8]

In 1990, antihunters in California used another

method. They proposed a state initiative, Proposition 117, that would ban the hunting of mountain lions in the state forever. The only exception was to be in cases where the animals threatened people or domestic animals. Proposition 117 was passed in November 1990 by a margin of 52 to 48 percent. Antihunting groups in other states have been encouraged by these results. According to one hunting writer, similar proposals were being considered in eleven other states in 1990.[9]

. . . AND HOW HUNTERS RESPOND

Hunters are, of course, angry about actions such as these. They complain that wildlife management policy is being made by people who don't know anything about the subject: the courts and the general public. One state official has stated that "allowing the public to decide the management of mountain lions was like allowing plumbers to do brain surgery."[10]

Another wildlife official pointed out that "mountain lion populations [are] at higher densities now than we ever thought possible." That suggests, he said, that the species is not even threatened, much less endangered, in the state and that Proposition 117 was simply unnecessary and wrong.[11]

Hunting groups cite example after example of this pattern. Antihunters make their case that "Bambi" and "Smoky the Bear" are being murdered by hunters. As a result, they sway popular opinion against well-established wildlife management techniques. What we're seeing, hunters say, is a century of wise, scientific wildlife management methods being abandoned in favor of "fuzzy wuzzy thinking about animal rights." The only hope for salvaging the kind of hunting that exists in the United States today, many hunters say, is to better educate the American public as to what hunting is *really* like.

THE CASE FOR HUNTING . . .
AND THE
ARGUMENTS AGAINST IT

How can anyone justify killing an animal? Many people feel that such an act simply *cannot* be justified. But hunters say that their sport can be justified on a number of bases: It provides an opportunity for people to be together and enjoy the great outdoors; it contributes to the preservation of many types of animals; it is a way of controlling predators; and it is a natural, instinctive behavior that provides an almost mystical feeling of accomplishment for the hunter.

"HUNTING IS A FORM OF OUTDOOR RECREATION . . ."

"I don't care if I get a deer and neither do my friends. Being outside, tramping the hedgerows on a crisp morning. That's as important as shooting something. Killing is only a tiny part of the overall experience."[1] That is the way one college student describes his reason for hunting. It is a social experience that provides companionship and the joy of being in contact with nature.

People who try to explain why they hunt often

use this argument. Especially among "naturalistic" hunters, those for whom hunting is a way of returning to a simpler, more natural way of life, this seems to be a primary motivation. They, along with other types of hunters, tend to play down the actual killing of their prey. One of the most famous phrases in all of hunting literature is "we kill to hunt, not the other way around."[2] That phrase means that hunters are really attracted by the beauties of nature, by the "ritual and tradition" of their sport, in which "killing involves only a split second."[3] Simply being out of doors with another hunter can be an "almost spiritual experience."[4]

Again and again, hunters talk and write about the sacredness of nature and the special feelings they have when they are outdoors. This theme runs throughout Jose Ortega y Gasset's *Meditations on Hunting,* perhaps the most famous book on hunting ever written. At one point he says, "This is the reason men hunt. When you are fed up with the troublesome present, with being 'very twentieth century,' you take your gun, whistle for your dog, go out to the mountain, and, without further ado, give yourself the pleasure during a few hours or a few days of being 'Paleolithic.' "[5]

Articles sometimes describe experiences during which a hunter encounters a particularly admirable animal and then decides not to kill it. Such decisions, one writer claims, are "born of respect, respect for life and living." That writer goes on to say that "if that seems a paradox in one who has chosen to hunt and kill, it's no less true."[6]

. . . AND HOW ANTIHUNTERS RESPOND

Antihunters are not willing to accept this argument. They point out that millions of people enjoy the outdoors by hiking, bird-watching, photography, and other activities that don't result in the death of animals. If the real joy of hunting is contact with nature, they say, why don't hunters shoot animals with cameras instead of guns?

"HUNTING IS A METHOD OF WILDLIFE CONSERVATION . . ."

Hunters also take credit for the fact that many forms of wildlife have flourished in North America during the twentieth century. They are the original and still the most concerned conservationists, they argue. Without the political activities and money provided by individual hunters and hunting groups, many animals would long ago have become extinct.

A promotional booklet for Safari Club International claims that "hunters are the original wildlife conservationists and we put our time and our money on the line to prove it."[7] The booklet goes on to argue that "habitat and herds must be kept in balance, and we believe that wisely managed hunting is one of the best ways to accomplish this."[8]

The Wildlife Legislative Fund of America makes a similar argument. "Sportsmen care deeply about wildlife and the environment," the organization says, "and have long been the foremost conservationists in this country. . . . Sportsmen remain the chief supporters of programs to preserve habitat and protect wildlife. Through license fees and special excise taxes on their equipment, they have already contributed more than $5 billion to the conservation cause."[9]

The financial contributions that hunters make to conservation come primarily through Pittman-Robertson taxes. In 1989, hunters paid $517 million for licenses, duck stamps, and excise taxes on equipment and ammunition.[10] Since 1937, these taxes have produced more than $1.7 billion in conservation funds.[11] Hunters remind us that the vast majority of this money goes back to states for improved conservation programs.

The National Rifle Association also talks about the role of hunting in conservation. In its *Hunting and Outdoor Skills Manual,* it tells young readers that hunters and conservationists have worked together to pass laws to protect animals and their habitat. "Today, wise game management and the millions of dollars provided by hunters through *hunting license* fees and conservation programs have saved many animal species from extinction."[12]

One wildlife authority has written that hunting is a perfectly natural human activity, a normal predator–prey relationship. Rather than be concerned about this reality, he says, we should be glad that humans are a "compassionate species, the only one." Under the conditions of modern society, "hunting and trapping work out best" for the management of other animals.[13]

Another hunter-writer has described the specific, direct contribution he makes to conservation of wildlife. On his own property last year, he says, "I raised 5,000 valley quail. I killed 49 of them. This reflects a traditional value of giving more to the land and environment than you take from it. How many antihunters," he asks, "can make a similar claim?"[14]

Traditionally, most groups interested in conservation were sympathetic to hunting. In his 1974 book against hunting, *Man Kind?,* Cleveland Amory wrote about the stranglehold that hunters had on virtually all major conservation and wildlife societies. He claimed that "there is hardly a single such society with the word 'wildlife' in it which is not hunter dominated."[15]

However, that pattern may be changing. Many

hunters now feel that conservation groups do not support hunting as vigorously as they ought to. In 1990, an editor of *Outdoor Life* magazine evaluated the stance of various conservation groups with respect to their views on hunting. He claimed that many conservation groups that were once "firmly dedicated" to hunting no longer look like "such sure-fire bets" in that regard.[16] In particular, he pointed a finger at the National Wildlife Federation (NWF). He says that, although the NWF is officially on record as supporting hunting as a conservation method, the organization "has actually come out on the opposition's side" in recent years.[17] He also lists the National Audubon Society, Nature Conservancy, World Wildlife Fund, and Wilderness Society as "fence straddlers" on the issue of hunting, and the Sierra Club as "leaning toward the antihunters."[18] In contrast, a number of other groups can safely be regarded as supportive of hunting for the purpose of conservation or other purposes. Among these are the National Rifle Association, the Wildlife Legislative Fund of America, and the International Shooting & Hunting Alliance.

Finally, the author lists a large number of conservation and wildlife organizations that are clearly antihunting. This list includes the Defenders of Wildlife, Friends of Animals, Greenpeace, Mobilization for Animals, and World Society for the Protection of Animals.[19]

. . . AND HOW ANTIHUNTERS RESPOND

Some critics reject the conservationist arguments of hunters. One writer claims that sportsman's conservation is a contradiction in terms. "What that really means," she says, "is that 'We protect things now so that we can kill them later' or 'Don't kill them all, just kill most of them.' "[20] A *Time* editorialist argues that "hunters are pests. Their blather about improving wildlife is mostly self-serving."[21]

The issue of Pittman-Robertson funds is not all that difficult, some antihunters say. Why not charge fees on other forms of outdoor recreation, such as a tax on binoculars or entry fees at wildlife refuges? With ten times as many nonhunters as hunters, we could easily be able to recover any Pittman-Robertson funds lost by a hunting ban.

"KILLING ANIMALS IS PLEASURABLE . . ."

The act of killing an animal is the single most controversial feature of hunting. Those who write in support of hunting typically agonize over this act. Some argue that, until the hunter fires a gun or shoots an arrow, there is relatively little difference between people who call themselves hunters and those who are nonhunters. Both love nature and respect its creatures. Out of this philosophy has come the "kill to hunt" philosophy described earlier.

Still, the act of killing is an absolutely essential part of hunting. With no killing, there would be no hunting. Thus, many hunters have turned around the "we kill to hunt" philosophy and say that "we hunt to kill." In other words, the point of hunting is not wildlife conservation or companionship or love of nature but the death of an animal.

One of the clearest statements of this philosophy appears in an essay by Humberto Fontova, a Louisiana wildlife writer: "Just once. My God, just once, I'd like to see hunters face up to the primal instinct that motivates us. . . . Essentially we are killers of animals in the most direct way and what distinguishes us from everyone else who indirectly causes animals to die is that we take delight in it. . . . We *like* to kill animals."[22]

Fontova takes issue especially with outdoors magazines that "constantly harp on sportsmanship, challenge, conservation ethics, nature worship, tradition, and camaraderie" in their editorials and then fill the rest of their pages with "guided hunts where, almost literally, all the hunter does is pull the trigger."[23] Fontova defends hunting as a "predatory instinct to kill." He believes that humans have been predators for tens of thousands of years. Eventually, he believes, that trait will be bred out of us. For his own part, Fontova says, "Thank God I won't be around by then."[24]

Many hunters have written about this so-called primal instinct to kill. One thoughtful essayist argues that "the necessity for a kill is never easily explained by one who hunts." For this writer, however, these urges and emotions "spring from instinct as honestly and purely as do the wiles of the chosen quarry."[25] In other words, hunters are, in some important ways, not so very different from the animals they hunt.

Another essayist echoes this view. "In nature," he writes, "every species, no matter how big or small, is either predator or prey, the hunter or hunted." This fact, he says, "is the dynamic of existence on our planet."[26]

In some cultures and some instances, the naturalness of killing is made abundantly clear. In the documentary film *In the Blood,* a father smears his eleven-year-old son's forehead with the blood of the first buffalo the son has ever killed. "Today you were part of nature," the father tells his son.[27]

Anyone who reads hunting magazines knows that, whatever the philosophers may say, many hunters are thrilled by the act of killing. Any number of stories recount the excitement of tracking down an animal and killing it.

At the conclusion of a well-balanced, thoughtful

117

article dealing with the antihunting dispute, an author describes her one and only hunting experience:

> My rifle crept to my shoulder. My pounding heart drove the sight in a circle around the doe's heart. Aeons passed before I steadied the barrel and fired. She flinched, ran a few steps, and collapsed. As I approached to deliver the last shot, her brown eyes glazed with mute reproach. I barely felt the kick or heard the roar of the rifle this time, but I turned cold suddenly as I bent to make the first incision.
>
> The doe's innards warmed my hands, and while I worked through the day, gutting her, hauling her home, skinning her carefully, butchering laboriously, and, finally, tasting the grilled meat, I began to feel—corny as it may sound—redeemed.

The lesson she learned from this experience, she said, was that

> for some perfectly sane, law-abiding people, hunting instills the same awe and respect for nature that others might feel scaling a glacier or surfing the aftermath of a Pacific storm. Hunting takes us out of the world of telephones, fluorescent lights, and bus exhaust into a primal world where, yes, the drama of the kill, the smell of the prey, and the feel of warm blood help restore our sense of belonging to nature.[28]

. . . AND HOW ANTIHUNTERS RESPOND

Antihunters would argue with many of the points hunters make about the act of killing an animal. To begin with, critics point out how differently humans view the act of killing from the way it affects game animals. From the hunter's standpoint, Joy Williams says, killing is "just a tiny part of the experience."

118

But for the animals, she points out, "the killing part is of considerably more importance."[29]

Antihunters also disagree with Humberto Fontova that human hunters are any longer a part of the great natural system of predator and prey. Luke Dommer, head of the Committee to Abolish Sport Hunting, points out that, in nature, predators normally remove older, sick, or otherwise unfit animals, leaving only the healthier, stronger individuals to breed. In this way, predators actually improve the condition of a prey population. In contrast, human hunters try to kill only the strongest animals. As a result, Dommer argues, a lot of inferior game animals are reproducing, resulting in weaker populations.[30]

Dommer also explains why human hunters don't look or act like natural predators. "When they go into the woods," he writes, "they have makeup on, they have camouflage suits, they wear red caps to protect themselves, they have binoculars, scopes, compasses, heating pads, electric socks, freeze-dried doe droppings, and even camouflaged toilet paper to keep them from being mistaken for white-tailed deer. They don't resemble natural predators at all. It's just the opposite."[31]

Finally, most antihunters would agree with Fontova about the role of killing in the hunt. In fact, Fontova's attitude is often their strongest argument *against* killing. Antihunters simply disagree with hunters about the morality and ethics of killing another animal. They do not accept the fact that killing is some glorious experience that is permissible simply because humans are stronger, smarter, or better equipped than other animals. Antihunters use phrases such as "mindless savagery," "heartless indifference,"[32] and "mass murder"[33] to describe the killing that occurs during hunting. The antihunting organization Friends of Animals calls the hunter "some-

119

what sadistic." "It takes a certain amount of sadism," the organization says, "to enjoy the death throes of a dying animal." [34] Luke Dommer agrees that "hunters get a real thrill from killing. I've seen guys after a kill," he writes, "who are flushed with a pinkish hue, glassy eyed, like they had been injected with some kind of drug. Many hunters are sick people in my opinion." [35]

At the most basic level, the debate over hunting comes down to the question of killing. Other issues aside, do humans have the right to take the life of another animal just for the pleasure it brings? On the one side, most hunters say yes, they are engaged only in a very old tradition of predator against prey. On the other side, antihunters say no, all forms of life are sacred, and a human must have some good reason, other than pure pleasure, to kill another animal.

The majority of North Americans are probably somewhere in between on this debate. They find reasons to both support and oppose hunting under various circumstances. How effectively pro- and anti-hunters can make their case to the large number of uncommitted nonhunters may well shape the future of this old sport in North America in the next century.

SOURCE NOTES

CHAPTER ONE

1. Erich Hobusch, *Fair Game: A History of Hunting, Shooting, and Animal Conservation* (New York: Arco, 1980), p. 19.
2. Hobusch, p. 16. See also Gunnar Brusewitz, *Hunting* (New York: Stein and Day, 1967), pp. 14–25.
3. Hobusch, pp. 14–20.
4. Conrad Phillip Kottak, *Cultural Anthropology*, 2nd edition (New York: Random House, 1979), pp. 237–238.
5. The Editors of *Life*, *The Epic of Man* (New York: Time, Inc., 1961), p. 50.
6. William H. Sebrell, Jr., James J. Haggerty, and the Editors of Time-Life Books, *Food and Nutrition* (New York: Time-Life, 1967), p. 34.
7. Editors of *Life*, *The Epic of Man*, p. 54.
8. Hobusch, p. 45.
9. Hobusch, p. 46.
10. Basil Davidson and the Editors of Time-Life Books, *African Kingdoms* (New York: Time, Inc., 1966), p. 114.
11. Hobusch, p. 48.

12. Hobusch, pp. 50–51.
13. Jacques Soustelle, *Daily Life of the Aztecs* (New York: Macmillan, 1955), p. 158.
14. Soustelle, p. 158.
15. Lucien Biart, *The Aztecs* (Chicago: A. C. Mc-Clurg, 1887), pp. 263–264.
16. Biart, p. 264.
17. Hobusch, p. 72.
18. Hobusch, p. 72.
19. Hobusch, p. 72.
20. Brusewitz, p. 113.
21. *The New Encyclopedia Britannica* (Chicago: University of Chicago, 1990), under "Hunting."
22. Brusewitz, p. 47.
23. Hobusch, p. 77.
24. Hobusch, p. 79.
25. Brusewitz, pp. 40–41.
26. Hobusch, p. 205.
27. Hobusch, p. 222.
28. Hobusch, pp. 221–222.

CHAPTER TWO

1. Peter Matthiessen, *Wildlife in America* (New York: Viking Penguin, 1987), p. 58.
2. Marshall B. Davidson, *Life in America* (Boston: Houghton Mifflin, 1951), p. 45.
3. Department of Conservation, School of Natural Resources, University of Michigan, *Hunting in the United States—Its Present and Future Role* (Washington D.C.: U.S. Government Printing Office, 1961), p. 5.
4. Joseph M. Petulla, *American Environmental History* (San Francisco: Boyd & Fraser, 1977), p. 39.
5. Petulla, p. 40.
6. Peter Verney, *Animals in Peril* (Provo, Utah: Brigham Young University, 1979), pp. 46–49.
7. Petulla, p. 40.

8. Matthiessen, p. 77.
9. *Hunting in the United States,* p. 6.
10. *Hunting in the United States,* p. 6.
11. Matthiessen, p. 162.
12. Quoted in Matthiessen, p. 158.
13. Matthiessen, pp. 159–160.
14. Genesis 1:28; also see Psalms 8:6–8.
15. See, for example, Michael W. Fox, *Returning to Eden: Animal Rights and Human Responsibility* (New York: Viking, 1980), chap. 1.
16. Erich Hobusch, *Fair Game: A History of Hunting, Shooting, and Animal Conservation* (New York: Arco, 1980), p. 176.
17. Fox, p. 194.
18. Fox, pp. 35–36.
19. The Editors of *Life, The Epic of Man* (New York: Time, Inc., 1961), p. 248.
20. Hobusch, p. 176.
21. Hobusch, pp. 174–175.
22. Petulla, p. 136.
23. Verney, p. 64.
24. Verney, pp. 66–67.
25. Verney, p. 67.
26. Matthiessen, p. 149.
27. Davidson, p. 50.
28. Matthiessen, p. 149.
29. Matthiessen, p. 161.
30. *Hunting in the United States,* p. 7.
31. John G. Mitchell, *The Hunt* (New York: Knopf, 1980), p. 101.
32. Mitchell, p. 101.
33. Mitchell, p. 105.
34. Keith McCafferty, "The Promised Land," *Field and Stream,* January 1990, p. 49.
35. McCafferty, p. 89.
36. Jim Zumbo, "West Deer Hunting 1990," *Outdoor Life,* September 1990, p. 133.

CHAPTER THREE

1. John G. Mitchell, *The Hunt* (New York: Knopf, 1980), p. 129.

2. Peter Wild, *Pioneer Conservationists of Western America* (Missoula, Mont.: Mountain Press, 1979), p. 55.

3. William L. Robinson and Eric G. Bolden, *Wildlife Ecology and Management* (New York: Macmillan, 1984), p. 413.

4. Robinson and Bolden, p. 9.

5. Robinson and Bolden, p. 9.

6. Robinson and Bolden, p. 17.

7. Department of Conservation, School of Natural Resources, University of Michigan, *Hunting in the United States—Its Present and Future Role* (Washington D.C.: U.S. Government Printing Office, 1961), p. 38.

8. Michael Satchell, "Refuge Hunting: Perverse Use or Logical Harvest?" *U.S. News & World Report*, January 12, 1987, p. 26.

9. Robinson and Bolden, p. 153.

10. Margaret L. Knox, "In the Heat of the Hunt," *Sierra*, November/December 1990, p. 51.

11. Robinson and Bolden, pp. ix–xiv.

12. Robinson and Bolden, pp. 277–278.

13. Knox, p. 51.

14. As quoted in Michael W. Fox, *Returning to Eden: Animal Rights and Human Responsibility* (New York: Viking, 1980), p. 47.

15. Joy Williams, "The Killing Game," *Esquire*, October 1990, p. 118.

16. Satchell, p. 26.

17. Michael Satchell, "The American Hunter Under Fire," *U.S. News & World Report*, February 5, 1990, p. 34.

18. Satchell, "Refuge Hunting," p. 26.

19. J. A. Miller, "Wildlife Refuge System: Refuge for Whom?" *Science News*, March 22, 1986, p. 183.
20. Miller, p. 183.
21. Miller, p. 183.
22. Satchell, "Refuge Hunting," p. 26.
23. Lonnie Williamson, "Wildlife *Mis*management," *Outdoor Life*, November 1989, p. 29, and Richard Conniff, "Fuzzy-Wuzzy Thinking About Animal Rights," *Outdoor Life*, February 1991, pp. 69ff.
24. Williamson, p. 30.
25. George Reiger, "The Resource Revolution," *Field and Stream*, June 1988, p. 14.
26. Reiger, p. 14.
27. Reiger, p. 16.
28. Reiger, p. 16.
29. Reiger, p. 16.
30. Reiger, p. 16.

CHAPTER FOUR

1. William L. Robinson and Eric G. Bolden, *Wildlife Ecology and Management* (New York: Macmillan, 1984), p. 412.
2. Peter Matthiessen, *Wildlife in America* (New York: Viking Penguin, 1987), p. 303.
3. Hunting laws and regulations were taken from the 1990–91 brochures for all states mentioned except Arizona, whose 1991–92 regulations were used.
4. John Gierach, "White World, Black Powder," *Field and Stream*, March 1991, p. 32.
5. U.S. Department of the Interior, Fish and Wildlife Service, *1985 National Survey of Fishing, Hunting, and Wildlife Associated Recreation* (Washington, D.C.: U.S. Department of the Interior, 1988).
6. Matthiessen, pp. 188–189.
7. Robinson and Bolden, p. 401.

8. Margaret L. Knox, "In the Heat of the Hunt," *Sierra,* November/December 1990, p. 53.
9. Duncan Barnes, "Up Front," *Field and Stream,* August 1991, p. 5.
10. Michael Milstein, "The Quiet Kill," *National Parks,* May/June 1989, p. 24.
11. Milstein, p. 24.
12. Daniel Glick, "The New Killing Fields," *Newsweek,* July 23, 1990, p. 54.
13. Eugene Linden, "Wildlife Cops on a Bust," *Time,* February 20, 1989, p. 18.
14. J. Skorupa, "High-tech War on Poachers," *Popular Mechanics,* July 1990, pp. 30–31.
15. William Brewer, "Undercover!" *The Conservationist,* January/February 1990, pp. 14–19.
16. Robinson and Bolden, p. 397.
17. *1990 California Hunting Regulations,* (Sacramento: Department of Fish and Game, 1990), p. 1.
18. Dan Sisson, "Grandpa and the Kid," *Field and Stream,* October 1991, p. 99.
19. The Wildlife Legislative Fund of America, *Update,* Winter 1991, Columbus, Ohio: The Wildlife Legislative Fund of America, p. 1.
20. Michael Satchell, "The American Hunter under Fire," *U.S. News & World Report,* February 5, 1990, p. 31.
21. Knox, p. 58.
22. George Reiger, "Our Achilles' Heel," *Field and Stream,* January 1991, p. 9.

CHAPTER FIVE

1. Michael Milstein, "The Quiet Kill," *National Parks,* May/June 1989, p. 20.
2. Milstein, p. 22.
3. Milstein, p. 20.

4. Michael Tennesen, "Poaching, Ancient Traditions, and the Law," *Audubon,* July 1991, p. 91.
5. Tennesen, pp. 92–93.
6. Ted Williams, "Open Season on Endangered Species," *Audubon,* January 1991, p. 32.
7. Williams, pp. 32–33.
8. Williams, p. 26.
9. Williams, p. 26.
10. Williams, p. 33.
11. "Big Game Poaching: An Organized Crime," *Environment,* January 1990, p. 23.
12. "Poacher in Hot Water," *Outdoor Life,* October 1989, p. 12.
13. Williams, p. 30.
14. Marc Reisner, "Hunting with the Enemy," *San Francisco Chronicle,* June 16, 1991, p. 10. See also Reisner's *Game Wars: The Adventures of an Undercover Wildlife Agent* (New York: Viking, 1991).
15. Milstein, p. 25.
16. Tennesen, p. 94.
17. Tennesen, p. 95.
18. Tennesen, p. 95.
19. Daniel Glick, "The New Killing Fields," *Newsweek,* July 23, 1990, p. 55.
20. Milstein, p. 25.
21. Robert F. Jones, "Farewell to Africa," *Audubon,* September 1990, p. 53.
22. Jones, p. 104.
23. Frank Graham, "Ban Bankrupts the Far East's Ivory Carvers," *Audubon,* September 1990, pp. 64–65.
24. Jones, p. 53.
25. Marilyn Achiron, "Making Wildlife Pay Its Way," *International Wildlife,* September/October 1988, p. 50.
26. Achiron, p. 50.
27. Achiron, p. 49.

28. Margaret L. Knox, "Horns of a Dilemma," *Sierra*, November/December 1989, p. 60.

CHAPTER SIX

1. Unless otherwise indicated, all statistics in this section are taken from U.S. Department of the Interior, Fish and Wildlife Service, *1985 National Survey of Fishing, Hunting, and Wildlife Associated Recreation*, (Washington, D.C.: U.S. Department of the Interior, 1988).
2. Thomas A. Heberlein, "Stalking the Predator," *Environment*, September 1987, p. 8.
3. George Reiger, "Instinct and Reality," *Field and Stream*, September 1991, p. 15.
4. Stephen R. Kellert, *A Study of American Attitudes toward Animals*, Washington, D.C.: U.S. Fish and Wildlife Service, 1976.
5. Dan Sisson, "Why I Hunt," *Sierra*, November/December 1990, p. 51.
6. Cleveland Amory, *Man Kind?* (New York: Harper & Row, 1974), p. 141.
7. Amory, p. 139.
8. John G. Mitchell, *The Hunt*, (New York: Knopf, 1980), p. 33.
9. Michael Satchell, "The American Hunter under Fire," *U.S. News & World Report*, February 5, 1990, p. 33.
10. Quoted in Amory, p. 38.
11. Walter L. Prothero, "Six Methods for Mule Deer," *Outdoor Life*, September 1990, p. 120.
12. Heberlein, p. 9.
13. "Hunters Shot Caged Animals for a Fee, Probers Say," *San Francisco Chronicle*, April 25, 1991, p. A26.
14. Mitchell, p. 115.
15. Heberlein, p. 9.
16. Jim Moore, "Partners and Other Gifts," *Outdoor Life*, July 1991, pp. 58, 88.

17. Mitchell, p. 13.

18. Erich Hobusch, *Fair Game: A History of Hunting, Shooting, and Animal Conservation* (New York: Arco, 1980), p. 119.

19. See, for example, the NRA pamphlet *Semi-Automatic Firearms: The Citizen's Choice* (Washington, D.C.: National Rifle Association, 1989).

20. George Laycock, "How to Kill a Wolf," *Audubon,* July 1990, p. 46.

21. Laycock, p. 44.

22. Laycock, p. 48.

23. *1985 National Survey,* Appendix B.

CHAPTER SEVEN

1. From the film *In the Blood,* quoted in Nick S. Seifert, "In the Blood," *Outdoor Life,* April 1990, p. 106.

2. Albert Schweitzer, *The Teaching of Reverence for Life* (New York: Holt, Rinehart, and Winston, 1965), pp. 22–23.

3. Joseph Wood Krutch, "A Damnable Pleasure," *Saturday Review,* August 17, 1957, p. 8.

4. Michael Satchell, "The American Hunter under Fire," *U.S. News & World Report,* February 5, 1990, p. 35.

5. Joy Williams, "The Killing Game," *Esquire,* October 1990, pp. 113–114. Readers should be aware that hunters claim that Ms. Williams's article contains a number of factual errors in addition to a philosophical position with which they disagree. See, for example, David E. Petzal, "Joy Williams Hates *You!*" *Field and Stream,* December 1990, pp. 16–17.

6. Steve Ruggeri, "Why I Don't Hunt," *Sierra,* November/December 1990, pp. 52–53.

7. C. Adams, "Hunting: An American Tradition," *The American Hunter,* May 1982, pp. 16–17.

8. Charles Elton, "On the Nature of Cover," *Journal of Wildlife Management,* 1939, cited in William L.

Robinson and Eric G. Bolden, *Wildlife Ecology and Management* (New York: Macmillan, 1984), p. 273.

9. Margaret L. Knox, "In the Heat of the Hunt," *Sierra,* November/December 1990, p. 59.

10. William G. Tapply, "Who Speaks for People?" *Field and Stream,* June 1991, p. 98.

11. Robinson and Bolden, p. 272.

12. Satchell, p. 35.

13. Satchell, p. 35.

14. Michael Satchell, "Refuge Hunting: Perverse Use or Logical Harvest?" U.S. News and World Report, January 12, 1987, p. 26.

15. John G. Mitchell, *The Hunt* (New York: Knopf, 1980), p. 82.

16. Quoted in Mitchell, p. 82.

17. National Rifle Association, *Hunting and Outdoor Skills Manual* (Washington, D.C.: National Rifle Association, 1990), p. 10.

18. Knox, p. 51.

19. Satchell, p. 31.

20. Satchell, p. 34.

21. Satchell, p. 34.

22. Walter E. Howard, "Animal Rights vs. Hunters," *Outdoor Life,* April 1991, p. 111.

23. Satchell, p. 35.

24. Williams, p. 121.

25. Knox, p. 58.

26. Mitchell, p. 50.

27. National Rifle Association, pp. 7–8.

CHAPTER EIGHT

1. These examples are taken from Beverly Conner and John Leahy, "Hunter Harassment: Plaguing our American Heritage," *Outdoor Life,* October 1990, pp. 83–104, and Douglas Starr, "Hunter Sabotage," *Omni,* October 1984, pp. 20+.

2. Starr, p. 20.

3. Conner and Leahy, p. 88.
4. Conner and Leahy, pp. 88, 98.
5. Conner and Leahy, p. 88.
6. "Hunter Harassment Laws," *Outdoor Life*, October 1991, p. 94.
7. Conner and Leahy, p. 89.
8. Jim Matthews, "The Domino Effect," *Outdoor Life*, March 1991, p. 78.
9. Ralph P. Stuart, "A Case Against Hunting," *Outdoor Life*, March 1990, p. 1.
10. Matthews, p. 79.
11. Conner and Leahy, p. 94.

CHAPTER NINE

1. Michael Satchell, "The American Hunter under Fire," *U.S. News & World Report*, February 5, 1990, p. 31.
2. See, for example, George Reiger, "We Aren't Thoughtless Thugs," *U.S. News & World Report*, February 5, 1990, p. 34.
3. Reiger, p. 34.
4. Mike Gaddis, "Taking a Life," *Audubon*, November 1990, p. 111.
5. Jose Ortega y Gasset, *Meditations on Hunting* (New York: Charles Scribner's Sons, 1972), p. 134.
6. Gaddis, p. 110.
7. *A Profile of Safari Club International* (Tucson: Safari Club International, n.d.), p. 2.
8. *A Profile of Safari Club International*, p. 3.
9. Don L. Johnson, "The Battle for Hunting Rights," *Outdoor Life*, March 1987, p. 80.
10. Satchell, p. 33.
11. Margaret L. Knox, "In the Heat of the Hunt," *Sierra*, November/December 1990, p. 51.
12. National Rifle Association, *Hunting and Outdoor Skills Manual* (Washington, D.C.: National Rifle Association, 1990), p. 3.

13. Walter E. Howard, "Animal Rights vs. Hunters," *Outdoor Life,* April 1991, p. 111.
14. Dan Sisson, "Why I Hunt," *Sierra,* November/ December 1990, p. 51.
15. Cleveland Amory, *Man Kind?* (New York: Harper & Row, 1974), p. 64.
16. John Leahy, "Stand Up and Be Counted," *Outdoor Life,* October 1990, p. 96.
17. Leahy, p. 96.
18. Leahy, p. 96.
19. Leahy, p. 96.
20. Joy Williams, "The Killing Game," *Esquire,* October 1990, p. 124.
21. John Skow, "Heroes, Bears and True Baloney," *Time,* November 13, 1989, p. 122.
22. Humberto Fontova, "Why We Hunt," *Sierra,* November/December 1990, p. 54.
23. Fontova, pp. 54–55.
24. Fontova, pp. 54–55.
25. Gaddis, p. 111.
26. Sisson, p. 50.
27. Skow, p. 122.
28. Knox, p. 59.
29. Williams, p. 113.
30. Wayne Pacelle, "An Interview with Luke Dommer," *The Animals' Agenda,* January 1989, p. 7.
31. Pacelle, p. 7.
32. Amory, p. 17.
33. Williams, p. 118.
34. Quoted in Beverly Conner and John Leahy, "Hunter Harassment: Plaguing our American Heritage," *Outdoor Life,* October 1990, p. 91.
35. Pacelle, p. 8.

BIBLIOGRAPHY

Achiron, Marilyn. "Making Wildlife Pay Its Way." *International Wildlife*, September/October 1988, 46–51.

Brusewitz, Gunnar. *Hunting*. New York: Stein and Day, 1967.

Conner, Beverly, and John Leahy. "Hunter Harassment: Plaguing Our American Heritage." *Outdoor Life,* October 1990, 83–104.

Davidson, Basil, and the Editors of Time-Life Books. *African Kingdoms*. New York: Time, Inc., 1966.

Department of Conservation, School of Natural Resources, University of Michigan. *Hunting in the United States—Its Present and Future Role*. Washington, D.C.: U.S. Government Printing Office, 1961.

Editors of *Life*. *The Epic of Man*. New York: Time, Inc., 1961.

Fox, Michael W. *Returning to Eden: Animal Rights and Human Responsibility*. New York: Viking, 1980.

Gaddis, Mike. "Taking a Life." *Audubon,* November 1990, 108–111.

Heberlein, Thomas A. "Stalking the Predator." *Environment,* September 1987, 6–11+.

Hobusch, Erich. *Fair Game: A History of Hunting, Shooting, and Animal Conservation.* New York: Arco, 1980.

Howard, Walter E. "Animal Rights vs. Hunters." *Outdoor Life,* April 1991, 111.

Jones, Robert F. "Farewell to Africa." *Audubon,* September 1990, 50–60+.

Kellert, Stephen R. "A Study of American Attitudes toward Animals." Washington, D.C.: U.S. Fish and Wildlife Service, 1976.

Knox, Margaret, L. "Horns of a Dilemma." *Sierra,* November/December 1989, 58–67.

————. "In the Heat of the Hunt." *Sierra,* November/December 1990, 48–59.

Laycock, George. "How to Kill a Wolf." *Audubon,* July 1990, 44–48.

Matthews, Jim. "The Domino Effect." *Outdoor Life,* March 1991, 61+.

Matthiessen, Peter. *Wildlife in America.* New York: Viking Penguin, 1987.

McCafferty, Keith. "The Promised Land." *Field and Stream,* January 1990, 48–49+.

Miller, J. A. "Wildlife Refuge System: Refuge for Whom?" *Science News,* March 22, 1986, 183.

Milstein, Michael. "The Quiet Kill." *National Parks,* May/June 1989, 18–25.

Mitchell, John G. *The Hunt.* New York: Alfred A. Knopf, 1980.

Ortega y Gasset, Jose. *Meditations on Hunting.* New York: Charles Scribner's Sons, 1972.

Reiger, George. "The Resource Revolution." *Field and Stream,* June 1989, 14–16.

Robinson, William L., and Eric G. Bolen. *Wildlife Ecology and Management.* New York: Macmillan, 1984.

Satchell, Michael. "The American Hunter under Fire." *U.S. News & World Report,* February 5, 1990, 30–37.

———. "Refuge Hunting: Perverse Use or Logical Harvest? *U.S. News & World Report,* January 12, 1987, 26.

Skow, John. "Heroes, Bears and True Baloney." *Time,* November 13, 1989, 122.

Starr, Douglas. "Hunter Sabotage." *Omni,* October 1984, 20+.

Tennesen, Michael. "Poaching, Ancient Traditions, and the Law." *Audubon,* July 1991, 90–97.

U.S. Department of the Interior, Fish and Wildlife Service. *1985 National Survey of Fishing, Hunting, and Wildlife Associated Recreation.* (Washington, D.C.: U.S. Department of the Interior, 1988).

Verney, Peter. *Animals in Peril.* Provo, Utah: Brigham Young University Press, 1979.

Williams, Joy. "The Killing Game." *Esquire,* October 1990, 112–128.

Williams, Ted. "Open Season on Endangered Species." *Audubon,* January 1991, 26–35.

Williamson, Lonnie. "Wildlife *Mis*management." *Outdoor Life,* November 1989, 29–30.

INDEX

on age and sex of animals, 58–59
antihunting movement and, 108–10
enforcement of, 63–66, 73–76
first laws, 17–18
history of, 53–55
land ownership and, 54–55
national laws, 59–63
on number of animals killed, 55–56, 59
open and closed season, 57
protection for game animals, 33–34
state laws, 55–59, 64
violation of. *See* Poaching
weapons laws, 57–58
for wildlife management, 44–45
Lead shot, 101, 102
Leopards, 77
Leopold, Aldo, 41
Lewis, Jennifer, 49
Loeb, Bruce, 76
Louis the Pious, 18

McCafferty, Keith, 36
Mary of Canterbury, 19
Massachusetts Bay Colony, 22–23, 55

Meditations on Hunting (Ortega y Gasset), 112
Migratory birds, 60, 92–93
Mitchell, John, 88, 105
Mobilization for Animals, 115
Mongoose, 61
Montezuma, Emperor, 16
Morality of hunting, 98–100
Mountain lions, 110
Mountain men, 30
Muzzle-loaders, 57–58, 89

National Audubon Society, 115
National hunting laws, 59–63
National parks, 44
National Park Service, 67
National Rifle Association, 89, 102, 105, 114, 115
National Wildlife Federation, 115
Native Americans, 27–30, 69
Naturalistic hunters, 86–87, 112
Nature Conservancy, 115
Nelson bighorn sheep, 59

ABOUT THE AUTHOR

David E. Newton is a writer and lecturer who has published numerous books for young readers, including *Consumer Chemistry Projects for Young Scientists, Science Ethics, Science/Technology/Society Projects for Young Scientists, Taking a Stand Against Pollution,* and *The U.S. and Soviet Space Programs.*

Before retiring from full-time teaching, he was a professor of chemistry and physics. He lives in San Francisco.